Dream Cottages

Dream Cottages

25 Plans for Retreats, Cabins, and Beach Houses

Catherine Tredway

STOREY
BOOKS

*The mission of Storey Communications is to serve our customers
by publishing practical information that encourages personal independence
in harmony with the environment.*

Edited by Deborah Balmuth and Larry Shea

Art direction and cover design by Mark A. Bergin

Text design by Mark Tomasi

Book layout and production by Susan Bernier

Cover and interior illustrations and photographs by Catherine Tredway with the exception
of top photograph on page 145 by Giles Prett/SCI.

Indexed by Susan Olason, Indexes & Knowledge Maps

The information in this book is true and complete to the best of our knowledge. All recommen-
dations are made without guarantee on the part of the author or Storey Books. The author and
publisher disclaim any liability in connection with the use of this information. For additional
information, please contact Storey Books, Schoolhouse Road, Pownal, Vermont 05261.

Storey books are available for special premium and promotional uses and for customized editions.
For further information, please call Storey's Custom Publishing Department at (800) 793-9396.

Printed in Canada by Transcontinental Printing

10 9 8 7 6 5 4 3 2 1

Library of Congress Cataloging-in-Publication Data

Tredway, Catherine.
    Dream cottages: 25 plans for retreats, cabins, and beach houses/by Catherine Tredway.
       p. cm.
    ISBN 1-58017-372-1 (alk. paper)
    1. Cottages—Designs and plans. 2. Vacation homes—Designs and plans. I. Title.

NA7574 .T68 2001

728.7'2'0222—dc21   2001020637

PREFACE

In my fifteen years as a designer, I have created hundreds of cottages and recreational homes. My worldwide experience has taught me that most people want the same things when it comes to their getaway: a beautiful, peaceful environment; room for family and friends; and space to engage in relaxing activities and hobbies.

I encourage clients to consider their personal wishes when building a retreat, and I guess that's where the phrase "dream cottage" comes in. Most of us are so busy we don't allow ourselves to think about what we really want. Whether you're an artist who dreams of a scenic studio, a cook who would love a luxury kitchen, or a woodworker who likes to putter, there is something you wish for.

The fun is in the fantasy, but in this book I also describe the many practical considerations involved in building your own cottage. My exterior designs are largely inspired by historic properties across North America, timeless classics that are unlikely to date themselves. The interior plans and features, however, are quite different from those of cottages of old. These twenty-five plans are carefully designed for the way we live and play today, and together they present options to meet the needs of any family situation, favorite activity, or local environment.

I hope this guide can pave the way for inspirational ideas and well-informed decisions. Enjoy the journey and the feeling of pride that comes with building your own dream cottage.

— *Catherine Tredway*

CONTENTS

ACKNOWLEDGMENTS

To my children Dane, Codie, and Clancy — my inspiration.

To Bruce — thank you for your support and guidance.

To my family — you gave me courage and wings.

*To Giuseppe and the Franchina Family — 'a design'
in dedication of an honorable man and contractor.
May you go on to fulfill the cottage dreams you began together.*

*To the Azzopardi Family — as clients you sparked my imagination,
as people you've done something beautiful and amazing!*

*To all of the designers and contractors whose work
has inspired within this book a next generation of ideas.*

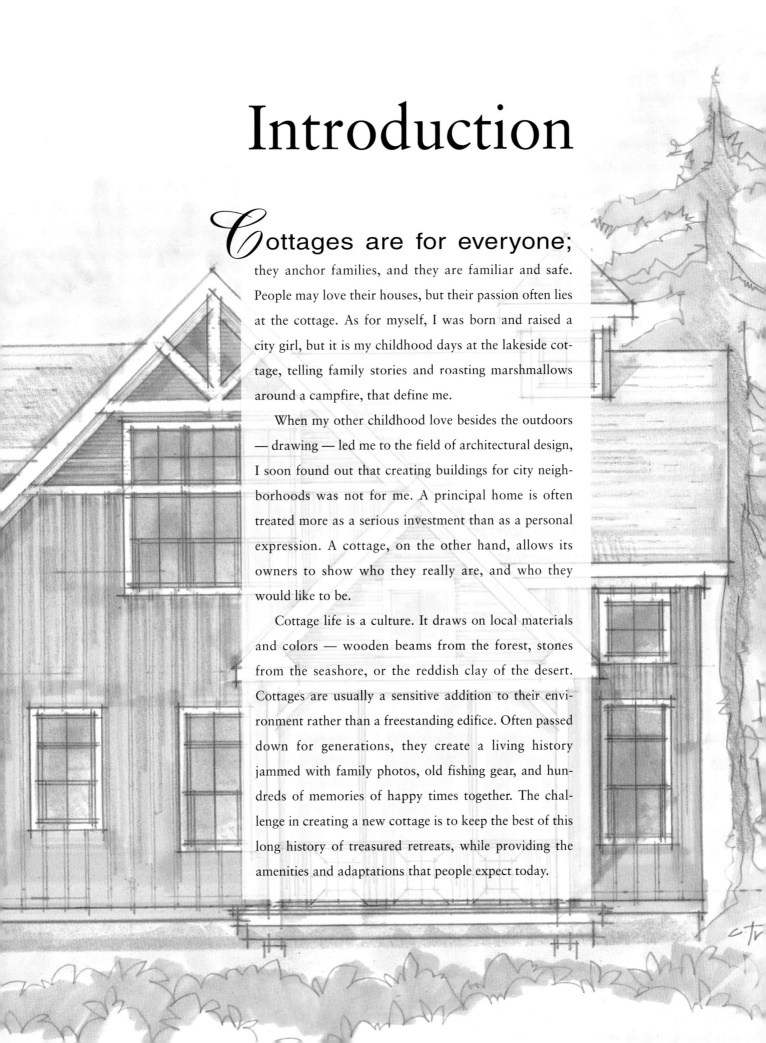

Introduction

Cottages are for everyone; they anchor families, and they are familiar and safe. People may love their houses, but their passion often lies at the cottage. As for myself, I was born and raised a city girl, but it is my childhood days at the lakeside cottage, telling family stories and roasting marshmallows around a campfire, that define me.

When my other childhood love besides the outdoors — drawing — led me to the field of architectural design, I soon found out that creating buildings for city neighborhoods was not for me. A principal home is often treated more as a serious investment than as a personal expression. A cottage, on the other hand, allows its owners to show who they really are, and who they would like to be.

Cottage life is a culture. It draws on local materials and colors — wooden beams from the forest, stones from the seashore, or the reddish clay of the desert. Cottages are usually a sensitive addition to their environment rather than a freestanding edifice. Often passed down for generations, they create a living history jammed with family photos, old fishing gear, and hundreds of memories of happy times together. The challenge in creating a new cottage is to keep the best of this long history of treasured retreats, while providing the amenities and adaptations that people expect today.

A Search for Tranquility

The earliest "cottages" belonged to the nobility of European countries. Weekend homes of great luxury afforded royal families the ability to spend time comfortably at an isolated site.

The first North American cottages were much more practical in nature. Cabins in the woods served as crude outposts for hunters and fishermen along the waterways of their nomadic existence.

Cottages as we know them today — weekend or summer retreats available to a great number of people — came about with the industrialization of the Victorian era. Building materials became readily available, and transportation was greatly improved. Extravagant summer homes, such as the grand "cottages" of Newport, Rhode Island, were the fashion of the day for the royalty of the industrial revolution.

Lodges were the common man's foot in the door, and properties of great opulence popped up everywhere. The weekend pilgrimage to the great outdoors had begun. A well-developed network of trains and boats transported guests from city locations to their

▲ The little house with ornate trim and quaint shutters, largely a development of the Victorian era, is what many people first think of when they hear the word "cottage."

weekend retreats. With cars and highways, access to these areas became even easier, and people began to branch out on their own.

After World War II, cottages became all the rage, and one by one select properties were gobbled up. The sheer volume and lack of guidelines brought many areas to the brink of ruining the beautiful, delicate environments that had caused the rush to build in the first place.

The 1960s brought more respect for the natural world around us. Since then, slowing development and stricter guidelines have finally begun to reverse some of the damage.

With limited availability, good recreational properties are coveted and have become very lucrative holdings. I purchased my first cottage in 1981 for $60,000; today the same property is worth more than ten times as much. Markets vary, but today's economy continues to find high value in these properties.

It is not wealth but wellness that seems to drive the current market. Baby boomers are the dominant consumers of real estate, and they are looking for a lifestyle with healthy, active leisure, as a contrast to their busy careers. Recreational properties center on family experiences, fitness, and sometimes even alternative working arrangements. The elusive goal is to find a tranquil spot that fulfills the many different needs of our complicated lives.

Making Dreams into Reality

While researching this book I traveled thousands of miles to recreational destinations all over North America, making note of various architectural and cultural influences. Throughout diverse landscapes and climates, the basic elements and culture of the cottage remained the same.

Dream Cottages provides a cross-section of these possibilities. Most of the designs are 1,200 to 1,800 square feet, and they represent a wide variety of styles. Keep in mind that any design choices in siding and features can be adapted to different local styles or needs.

Four major environments characterize the plans: Seaside, Lakeside, Mountain, and Prairie/Desert.

Seaside designs feature predominant water views. They have forward access to the ocean and rear access to the driveway. Different sides of the cottage and various vantage points take advantage of sun and wind conditions throughout the day.

Lakeside designs emulate many of the qualities of seaside properties but are geared for less sun and wind exposure. Most have screened porches to fend off bugs, which come hand-in-hand with the forest.

Mountain designs accommodate sloping lots. They maintain beautiful lines while maximizing captured space beneath the building, an important feature in colder climates.

Prairie/Desert designs greet wide-open spaces with extensive wraparound porches. These lower buildings are more wind resistant, and in the case of adobe buildings they remind us of some of the oldest local traditions.

In each of these environments, people have a strong desire for certain elements, such as "great rooms" for open concept living, main-floor master suites, private guest accommodations, or walk-in pantries. Naturally you will want to add your own personal twists. These twists may be practical or deliciously excessive.

I recommend that you consult with your local contractors and building material suppliers in order to develop a design that gives the best value for the money. Most people don't build their dream property with resale as a primary concern, but it should always be considered. All of these plans contain time-tested features popular in the real estate market.

The two pages that follow comprise the Cottage Planner, a concise questionnaire to guide you through

▲ A cheerful house by the ocean is one of the most common dreams of people looking for a cottage of their own.

the process of making decisions about features, styles, and budget-related issues. It is similar to the questions I ask of all clients when trying to determine what type of cottage will best fit their needs and lifestyle. I suggest supplementing this form with magazine clippings, photos, or anything that reminds you of the cottage you would like to someday own. In the earliest stages of a project, this planner can help you to evaluate potential properties; later on, you can use it to convey exactly what you want to an architect, designer, contractor, or real estate agent.

No one design in this book, or any book, could fulfill all the desires of someone looking for their own perfect cottage. As you look at the Cottage Planner, the designs for the twenty-five varied cottages that follow it, and the many photos of cottage features and styles that I have included, I hope that your own dream cottage will become more defined, better capturing what is important to you. And as you read the advice and practical information the book contains, I hope that this vibrant dream will start to move one step closer to reality.

THE COTTAGE PLANNER

Cottage Site

General vision (region; setting; landscape; nearness to other cottages, bodies of water, services):

_____

_____

_____

On a separate page, draw a diagram with a general vision for your imagined or actual site. Show driveway access, water access, best views, areas to avoid, and required setbacks. Attach survey if available.

Site access (water, foot, land, plane, etc.):_____

Landscape considerations (future landscape and garden plans, trees, drainage):_____

_____

Special considerations (easements, future construction): _____

_____

Permit/bylaw requirements: _____

Service locations (water, electric, septic, etc.): _____

_____

Please identify these items on site plan.

General Conditions

Budget/estimated square footage: _____

Proposed construction start date: _____ Targeted completion date:_____

People considerations (Who will use the cottage? Frequently or occasionally?): _____

_____

Style of living (formal or informal?):_____

Practical considerations (How will the occupants use the cottage?): _____

_____

Exterior Requirements

General requirements (architectural style, entries and windows, building shape and features):

_____

_____

On a separate sheet, sketch building styles and features you find attractive.

Window/door style: _____ Roofing material: _____

Siding material: _____ Porches, decks, patios: _____

Garage, carport, driveway: _____

Special construction or outbuildings: _____

Interior Requirements

Entries (locations, necessary facilities): _____
_____

Kitchen and Dining

General requirements (pantry, wine cellar, island, china storage, built-in appliances, broom closet):
_____
_____

Dining area (For how many? Separate dining room? Describe furniture and dimensions):
_____
_____

Bedrooms

General requirements (number, size, first or second floor): _____
_____

Master bedroom (Special requirements? Attached bathroom?): _____
_____
    Furniture and storage required: _____

Second bedroom: _____
    Furniture and storage required: _____

Additional bedrooms: _____
    Furniture and storage required: _____

Bathrooms

General requirements: _____
_____

Bath 1 (location, tub and/or shower, whirlpool): _____

Bath 2 (location, requirements as above): _____

Additional bathrooms: _____

Laundry and Mechanical

Washer/dryer/clothesline (location and requirements): _____

Mechanical systems (heating, hot water, air-conditioning): _____

Living Areas

General requirements (activities, numbers of people): _____

Main living area (size, seating, access to other areas): _____

Special features (fireplace, home theater, other): _____

Other specialized living spaces (hobby room, home office, spa, exercise room): _____
_____

Special mechanical or other requirements for above spaces: _____

ONE

A Lakeside Retreat

$\mathcal{T}$he **Rousseau House** is a place designed for family living, with large dining and living areas and multiple bedrooms and bathrooms. Cottage life spills from indoors to outdoors here, with plenty of spots to spend time together or to steal away for a private moment. My family loves movies, so I included a small home theater with stadium seating, a popcorn machine, and a coffee/juice bar. This "activity wing" could be customized to the interests of any family.

At first this may seem an impossibly expensive undertaking, but with resourceful planning it can be achieved for a reasonable cost. The focus is on small bedrooms, well-defined common and private living areas, large dining areas, and a private "host suite." Locker-room-style bathrooms for "boys" and "girls" add a fun camp flavor.

Building Style	Victorian (Ontario Vernacular)	**First Floor Area**	1,528 sq. ft.
Bedrooms	5	**Second Floor Area**	912 sq. ft.
Bathrooms	3½	**Total Floor Area**	2,440 sq. ft.

Front Elevation Features

- Dual front porches with French doors and full-length shutters
- Bracketed porch with decorative millwork
- Vertical stained wood siding
- Transoms above all main floor windows (traditional single-hung windows below)
- Quaint dormers

Rear Elevation Features

- Unusual glazing for window of second-floor bathroom
- French door grouping for master suite and living and dining areas
- Decorative railings

This cottage design

has been identified as Ontario Vernacular because of its simple detail and moderate decorative millwork, as shown in these examples from similar cottages. Over the years I have seen many perfectly fine buildings ruined by unrefined choices in their finishes. A properly "rustic" approach could include rough-sawn vertical siding, 6-inch frieze board and base trim, and simple king posts. The porches would have 8-inch-square posts or simple bold turnings with modest brackets. The "high Victorian" approach, on the other hand, can include almost any type of mill-work. The key is to choose details from the same period and to focus on quality, not quantity.

▲ Finely crafted posts on the porch.

▲ Multi-layered millwork in the dormers.

▲ Graceful brackets support a porch roof.

▲ An inviting wraparound porch with a series of French doors.

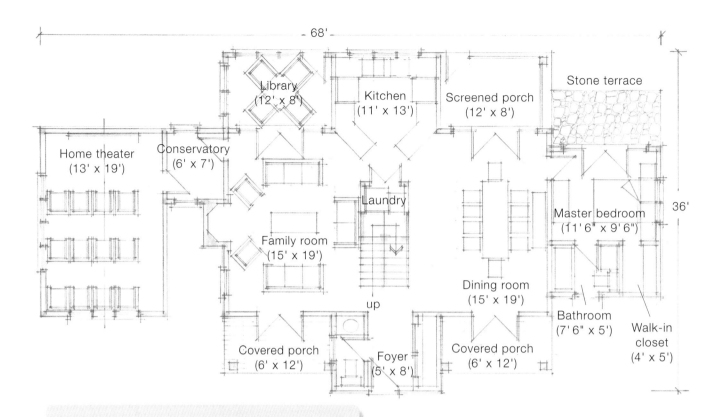

68'

36'

Library
(12' x 8')

Kitchen
(11' x 13')

Screened porch
(12' x 8')

Stone terrace

Home theater
(13' x 19')

Conservatory
(6' x 7')

Laundry

Master bedroom
(11' 6" x 9' 6")

Family room
(15' x 19')

Dining room
(15' x 19')

up

Bathroom
(7' 6" x 5')

Walk-in
closet
(4' x 5')

Covered porch
(6' x 12')

Foyer
(5' x 8')

Covered porch
(6' x 12')

First Floor Features

- Spacious foyer with closet and half bathroom

- Dining area with seating for twenty

- Family room with central fireplace

- Nine-foot ceilings

- Library and screened porch for private getaways

- Generous kitchen with adjoining laundry area

- Private host suite

- Conservatory (equipped with popcorn maker and refreshment area)

- Home theater with cathedral ceiling and stadium seating

▲ You might identify your hideaway with a hand-carved sign.

▶ In this example, a kitchen sunroom and a balcony off the master suite make great places for enjoying the view.

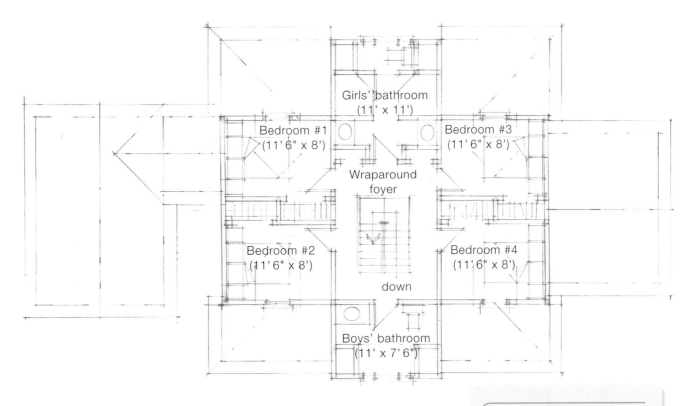

Girls' bathroom
(11' x 11')

Bedroom #1
(11' 6" x 8')

Bedroom #3
(11' 6" x 8')

Wraparound
foyer

Bedroom #2
(11' 6" x 8')

Bedroom #4
(11' 6" x 8')

down

Boys' bathroom
(11' x 7' 6")

Victorian architecture

originated in the 1830s and spread to many English-speaking countries during the reign of Queen Victoria. Weekend retreats were soon adorned with romantic and eclectic finishes, and the "little Victorian cottage" has become synonymous with this style.

Cottages of this type can be found throughout North America; it is the millwork features that define its local characteristics. These variations are what we mean by "vernacular": the local modification of a traditional style for reasons of culture, climate, or available materials. In the example shown on the facing page, a client approached me with a painting of a local historic building. We scaled down its original 6,000 square feet to 1,500 — a more suitable size for a retirement cottage. The owners reproduced much of the original detail while adding some personal flair.

▲ The owner of this Victorian cottage also owned the local wagon shop that milled the fine trim for this building and others in the area.

Family Compound
by the Sea

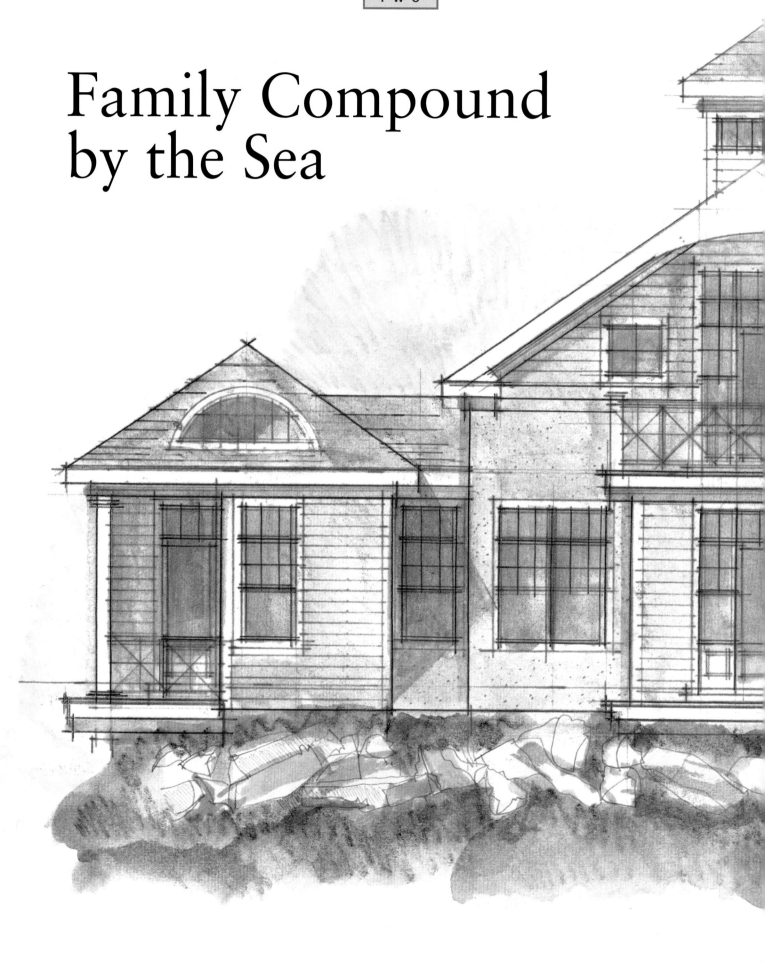

𝒯he Cove House is a sprawling cottage with room enough for several families to share. This is a dream for many of us, but these ventures can be complicated. With multiple ownership, disputes and hard feelings may arise. I recommend the following guidelines:

- Equal ownership by all parties involved.
- Distinct accommodation for each of the family groups.
- Democratic decisions related to exteriors, grounds, and common areas, and equally shared costs.

  With a positive approach and good communication, this mini-community can be the ultimate family experience.

Building Style	Shingle
Bedrooms	3
Bathrooms	3½
First Floor Area	1,882 sq. ft.
Second Floor Area	453 sq. ft.
Total Floor Area	2,335 sq. ft.

Rear Elevation Features

- View of all three pods
- Optional hip or gable roof on second floor
- Cupola open to second floor
- Eyebrow dormers on pods

Left Elevation Features

- Second-floor walk-out over main entry
- Shingle siding
- Optional gable end front and rear
- Generous window plan for each pod

▲ Fishing paraphernalia can inspire a color palette for interior and exterior finishes.

This group of cottages

(above) on the Massachusetts coast was my inspiration for the design of the Cove House. I love how the shingle finish blends with the coastal rock to form a hazy pastel completely at ease in the natural environment. To design and decorate a cottage that looks like it belongs, it is essential to take cues from the surroundings.

▲ The grill pattern of these fishing traps provides a subtle association when picked up in architectural features.

◄ Be sure the building is sited to make the most of local views.

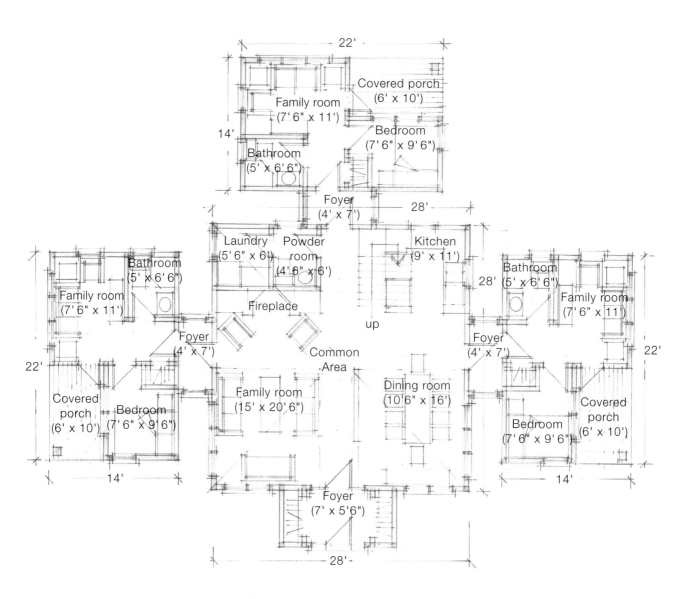

Family room (7' 6" x 11')

Covered porch (6' x 10')

Bedroom (7' 6" x 9' 6")

22'

14'

Bathroom (5' x 6' 6")

Foyer (4' x 7')

28'

Laundry (5' 6" x 6')

Powder room (4' 6" x 6')

Kitchen (9' x 11')

Bathroom (5' x 6' 6")

Family room (7' 6" x 11')

28'

Bathroom (5' x 6' 6")

Family room (7' 6" x 11')

Fireplace

up

Foyer (4' x 7')

Common Area

Foyer (4' x 7')

22'

22'

Covered porch (6' x 10')

Bedroom (7' 6" x 9' 6")

Family room (15' x 20' 6")

Dining room (10' 6" x 16')

Bedroom (7' 6" x 9' 6")

Covered porch (6' x 10')

14'

14'

Foyer (7' x 5'6")

28'

First Floor Features

Three individual "pods" each containing:

- A family room with pullout couch and fireplace
- Full bathroom
- Separate bedroom
- Covered porch
- Private entry
- Cathedral ceiling

A common area with:

- Laundry facilities and adjoining powder room
- Dining area for twenty
- Large family room with central fireplace
- Front foyer with generous closet space
- Partial cathedral ceiling over living and dining areas

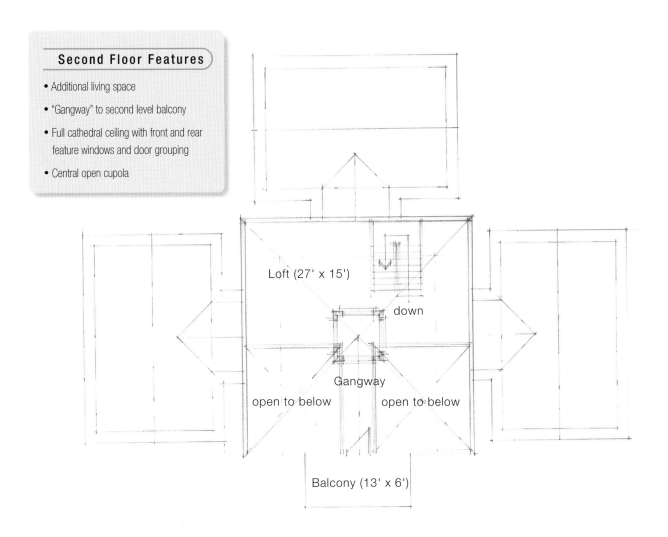

- Additional living space
- "Gangway" to second level balcony
- Full cathedral ceiling with front and rear feature windows and door grouping
- Central open cupola

Loft (27' x 15')

down

Gangway

open to below   open to below

Balcony (13' x 6')

A second home provides owners with a

chance to use less conventional approaches for personalizing. This is one of the things that draws me to recreational design; vacation homes are much less staid and more in tune with the personalities of their inhabitants. With almost every cottage I design or visit, I see signs of this in the choices of decorative art, paint finishes, and custom details. All are part of what might be called the unusual, but which I prefer to think of as the individual. It takes a good sense of humor and a little courage to go outside the norm, but it can lead to some fun results.

▲ Pick a fun name for your compound.

▶ Interior decoration in cottages is often rustic and whimsical.

THREE

An Artist's Shingle Cottage

$\mathcal{R}$ockport Cottage is a place where the cries of seagulls and a rocky shore strewn with seaweed come to life. Flat-topped dormers and covered porches are restful places for cold lemonade on a hot summer day. The traditional steep pitch of the roofline provides quaint but usable space. The windows are classically balanced, the horizontal siding is shingle, and small feature windows add a little nautical flair. This artist's retreat has a studio on the main floor with a dramatic cathedral ceiling. Inspirational views are easy to find from the second-floor balcony and the screened porch.

GENERAL FEATURES

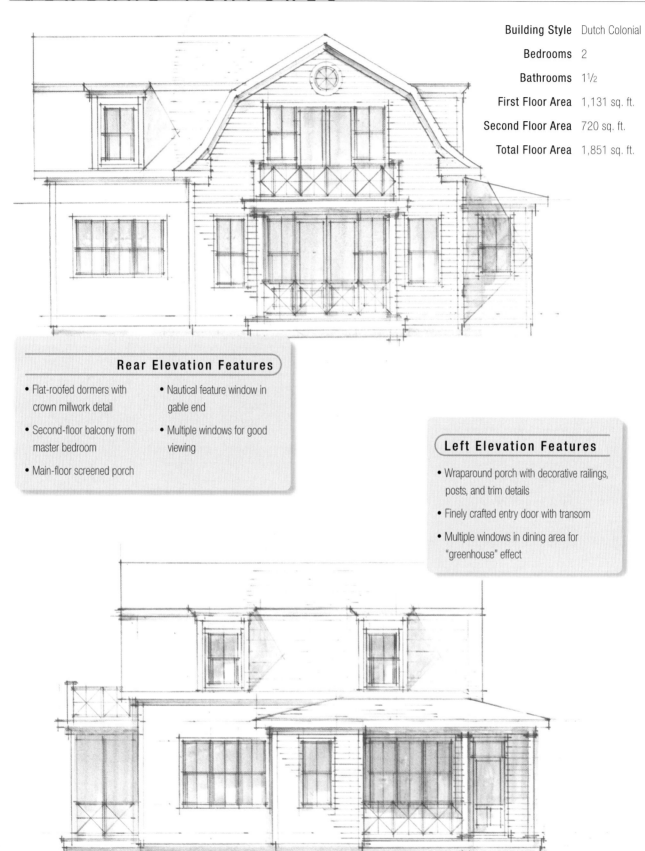

Building Style	Dutch Colonial
Bedrooms	2
Bathrooms	1½
First Floor Area	1,131 sq. ft.
Second Floor Area	720 sq. ft.
Total Floor Area	1,851 sq. ft.

Rear Elevation Features

- Flat-roofed dormers with crown millwork detail
- Second-floor balcony from master bedroom
- Main-floor screened porch
- Nautical feature window in gable end
- Multiple windows for good viewing

Left Elevation Features

- Wraparound porch with decorative railings, posts, and trim details
- Finely crafted entry door with transom
- Multiple windows in dining area for "greenhouse" effect

This example of a classic gambrel at left shows how the Dutch Colonial style can be finished with more formal features if desired. Note the subtle curve at the end of the roof as well as the classically trimmed dormer windows.

Opportunities abound for custom millwork details in the porch, railing, and dormer finishes. In a clean, traditional style such as this, ornamentation does not have to be elaborate or expensive to have a big impact. Extending the style throughout your landscape, as below, makes your property a cohesive whole.

▲ Fine detail in the window casings complements the traditional cladding.

▲ Simple millwork combinations can create a very high-end result.

▲ Plantings and garden structures enhance the architectural detail.

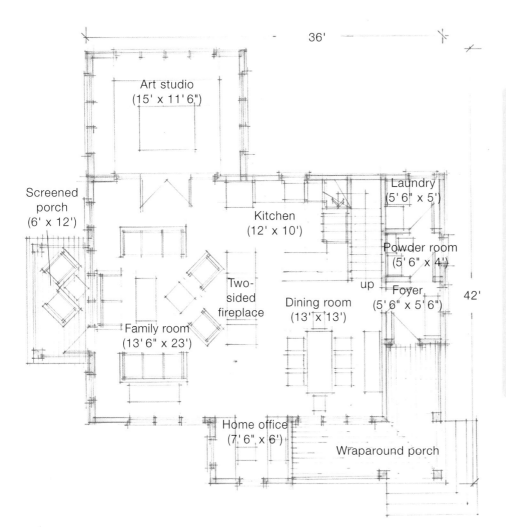

36'

Art studio
(15' x 11' 6")

Screened
porch
(6' x 12')

Kitchen
(12' x 10')

Laundry
(5' 6" x 5')

Powder room
(5' 6" x 4')

Two-
sided
fireplace

up

Dining room
(13' x 13')

Foyer
(5' 6" x 5' 6")

42'

Family room
(13' 6" x 23')

Home office
(7' 6" x 6')

Wraparound porch

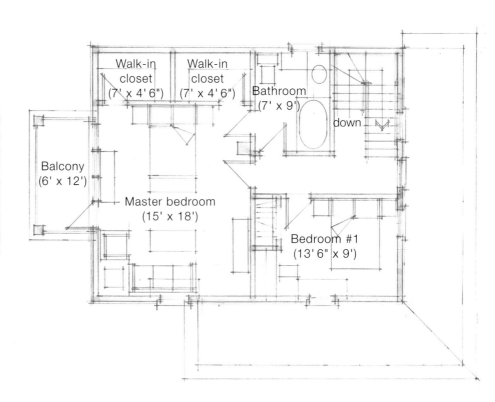

Walk-in
closet
(7' x 4' 6")

Walk-in
closet
(7' x 4' 6")

Bathroom
(7' x 9')

down

Balcony
(6' x 12')

Master bedroom
(15' x 18')

Bedroom #1
(13' 6" x 9')

Porches have always had cultural significance at recreational properties. Late night conversations and rainy evenings on the porch are some of my fondest memories of childhood summers at the cottage.

Porches serve as many things: secondary living rooms, shelter from bugs and rain, or even simply architectural features. They come in all shapes and sizes and can be open, screened, or three-season. When considering a porch for your recreational property, first ask yourself the following questions:

- Do weather conditions in my area make it necessary to have a shelter over the main entry?
- Do I need additional living or sleeping space?
- Is the area of the proposed porch vulnerable to hungry insects?
- Would I like to use this space year-round?
- How will a porch overhang affect the lighting inside the cottage, and is this a compromise I am willing to make?
- How will this architectural feature be complementary in both size and detail to the rest of the building?
- What outside views am I trying to capture? Will any views from inside rooms be limited by the porch?

Porches usually are open areas that take a beating from exposure and extreme weather conditions. They are often the first candidates for major renovation. Following are some important considerations to keep in mind during the initial construction.

- Make sure the foundation is on solid, undisturbed soil to the appropriate depth.
- Identify both current and potential uses. If you want to convert this screened porch to a sunroom at some point, build with this in mind.
- For screened porches, make sure all small openings are closed tight, as porches are favorite spots for wasps and small insects.
- Try to avoid sills and ledges, as these are also favorite nesting spots.
- Be certain that water from both the decking and the roof is properly draining away from the main structure.
- Consider the durability of the finish in all areas; try to avoid high-maintenance conditions.
- Make sure the post and railing millwork complement the rest of the structure. Their height and depth should also be proportionate.

▲ A screened porch can be supported on Sonotubes (concrete-filled fiber tubes) for warm-weather use only.

▶ A fully enclosed porch with foundation offers extensive views and year-round use.

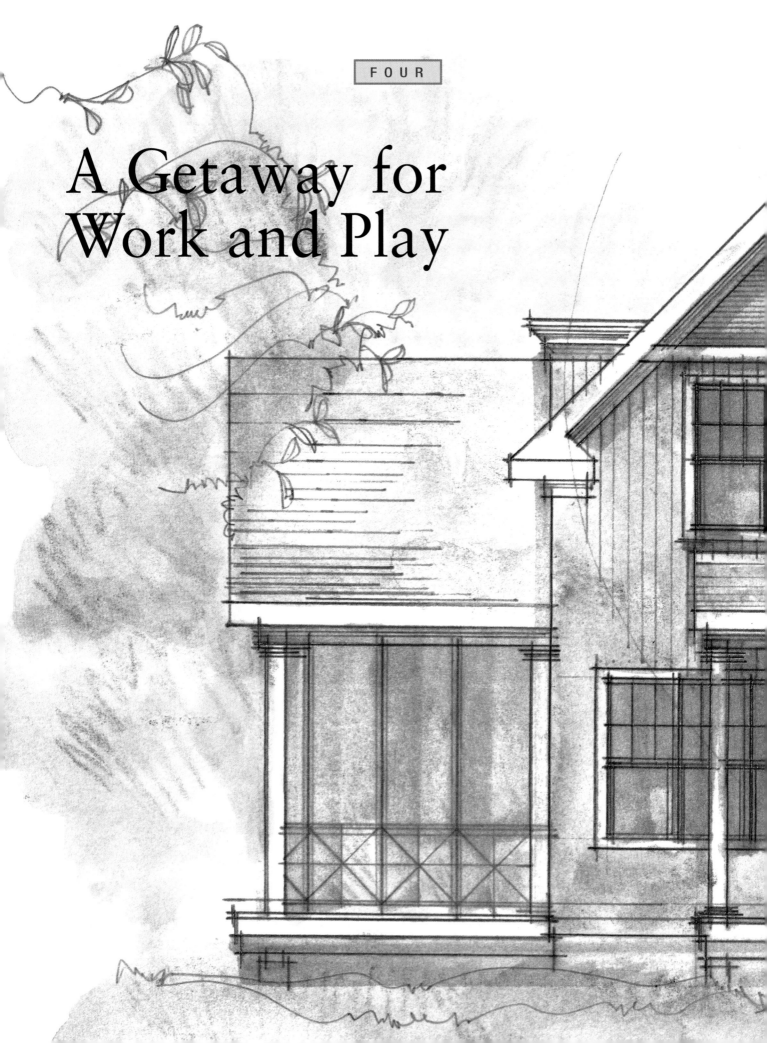

FOUR

A Getaway for Work and Play

The Oxford House

The Oxford House is a response to the rising trend of mobile offices. With satellites and cell phones, a fully equipped office can be anywhere we want it to be. More and more people are looking for alternatives that will provide a higher quality of living; the out-of-town office may be just the start they need.

When planning a home office, consider both your technological and your recreational requirements. I have created offices in the heart of the living areas, as well as those that are separate. The separate office allows for undivided attention to work, faster completion of tasks, and therefore more time for leisure. For myself, I prefer a private workspace with a scenic, peaceful view.

GENERAL FEATURES

Building Style	Colonial Revival	**First Floor Area**	1,074 sq. ft.
Bedrooms	3	**Second Floor Area**	768 sq. ft.
Bathrooms	1½	**Total Floor Area**	1,842 sq. ft.

Front Elevation Features

- Private entry to home office with an interesting angled door
- Private entry with bracketed porch
- Decorative grill pattern on double-hung windows
- Decorative railing detail on screened porch
- Flat-topped dormers
- Feature window in gable end

Left Elevation Features

- Flat-topped dormers provide generous lighting to bedroom and loft areas
- A full-length porch offers a wide-ranging view and easy access to outdoors
- Vertical V-joint siding and finely trimmed windows make an informal but classic finish

Classical trim details

featured in white, at left, provide a fine contrast and accentuate high-quality details. Like the Oxford House, the home pictured here is a relatively compact design that provides expansive internal space.

This house is also similar to the Oxford House in the full-length balcony accessible from a door on the second floor. In my design, this door leads from a loft space near the three bedrooms, making each of the upstairs rooms only a short walk from a refreshing outdoor stroll.

Your color choices

should reflect the local environment. These native grasses at right are in a peaceful, natural color similar to that of the house above and would be a perfect choice for the Oxford House.

Become familiar with the predominant natural colors and most common cottage finishes in your neighborhood. Bring local photos, or even leaves or other natural objects, with you to the paint store when making your finish choices.

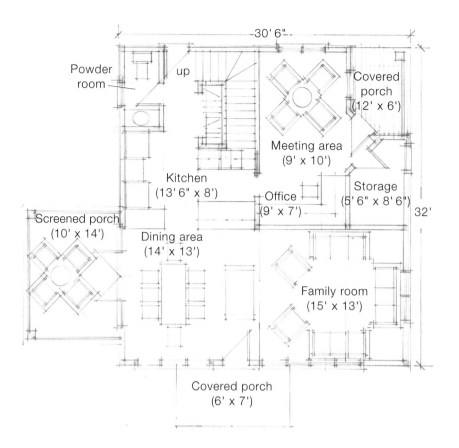

Powder room

up

Covered porch
(12' x 6')

Meeting area
(9' x 10')

Kitchen
(13' 6" x 8')

Office
(9' x 7')

Storage
(5' 6" x 8' 6")

Screened porch
(10' x 14')

Dining area
(14' x 13')

Family room
(15' x 13')

Covered porch
(6' x 7')

- 30' 6" -

32'

First Floor Features

- Separate office entrance near the driveway with a covered porch

- Meeting "pit" with scenic views

- Built-in smart-wired workstation with full computer capabilities

- Storage/filing room

- Private entry with covered porch

- Powder room

- Kitchen with seating island and built-in laundry facility

- Dining area for maximum of ten

- Two-sided fireplace opening to dining and living areas

- Living room with generous window area and cathedral ceiling above

- Screened porch with interesting millwork details

Second Floor Features

- Master bedroom with fireplace and French balconies over family room

- En suite bathroom with soaking tub

- Door to full-length balcony with views

- Two additional private bedrooms

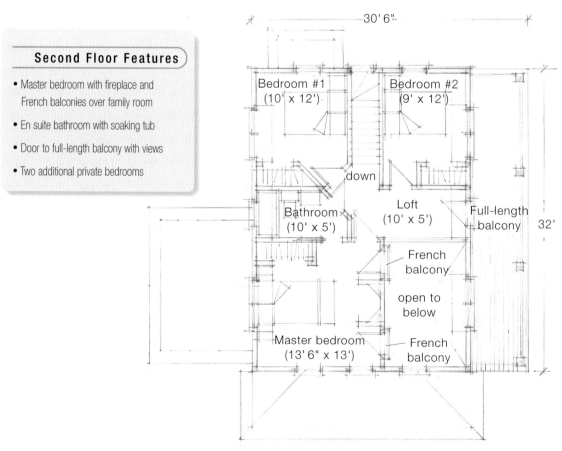

- 30' 6" -

Bedroom #1
(10' x 12')

Bedroom #2
(9' x 12')

down

Bathroom
(10' x 5')

Loft
(10' x 5')

Full-length balcony

32'

French balcony

open to below

Master bedroom
(13' 6" x 13')

French balcony

When deciding where to locate a cottage, take the following points into consideration:

• How can the best possible views be available from different parts of the cottage?
• Where is the best place to locate the driveway, considering local requirements, site services, natural lighting, and building design? (It is best to park as close to the front entry and kitchen as possible).
• Are there conditions such as slopes and rock that must be considered or worked around?
• Are there local conservation and bylaw restrictions that limit the boundaries of construction and clearing on the site?

These photos show the good results you can get when you place a building with an eye to creating optimal views and with careful consideration of the land's contours. Sometimes what might be seen as a conventional obstacle in the terrain will present an interesting opportunity. For example, sloping lots are a challenge when building the foundation, but they can allow for wonderful walk-out basements and underground parking areas.

▲ Take advantage of slopes to make the most of views or create walk-out basements.

▲ A wooded site can be difficult to build on, but trees add privacy.

FIVE

Weekend Workshop

The Settlement House is a

rustic log or log-style building perfect for the weekend carpenter or shop worker. The rooflines are traditional French-Canadian Vernacular. I see this cottage situated on a mountain lake in the Laurentians, or perhaps the Adirondacks. The cabin has a spacious living area with a stone fireplace. The screened porch could be glassed in for year-round use.

The workshop is suited for a variety of uses: car restoration, with a block and tackle mounted to the timber frame; woodworking with easy access through the double doors; or fine work such as carving and modeling. The shop could be heated with a gas or wood stove, and it has plenty of storage room on its second level.

Building Style	French-Canadian Vernacular	**First Floor Area**	1,232 sq. ft.
Bedrooms	2	**Second Floor Area**	594 sq. ft.
Bathrooms	1	**Total Floor Area**	1,826 sq. ft.

Rear Elevation Features

- Two dormers create interesting roofing and viewing from second-level bedrooms

- Spacious screened porch could be converted to year-round use

- Timber-frame porch posts

- Decorative railings provide custom touches

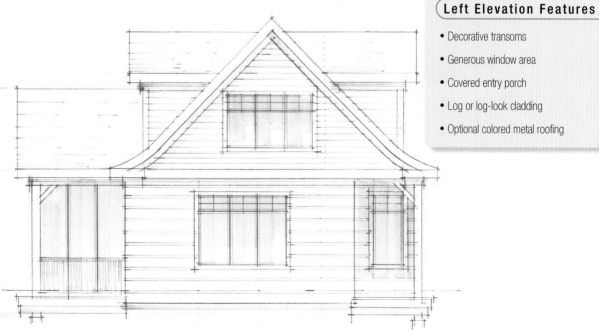

Left Elevation Features

- Decorative transoms

- Generous window area

- Covered entry porch

- Log or log-look cladding

- Optional colored metal roofing

▲ Folk art pieces may relate to a cottage's setting.

Architectural salvage yards and demolition firms are great sources for reclaimed building products. The craftsmanship of some of these older products makes them difficult and prohibitively expensive to duplicate. Architectural antiques provide instant warmth and conversation-starting focal points for many recreational sites.

▲ Use your imagination to find new uses for reclaimed, unusual pieces.

▲ Incorporating older architectural elements can bring a sense of history to a new cottage.

◄ Salvage-yard finds can be incorporated into both interior and exterior.

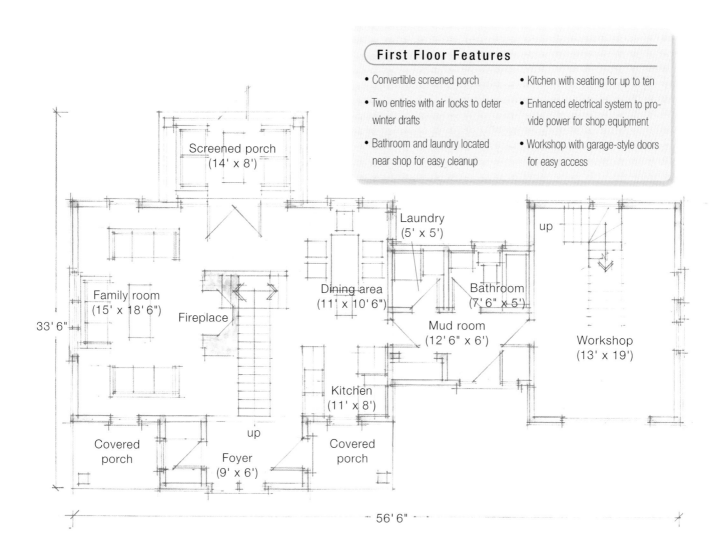

Screened porch
(14' x 8')

First Floor Features

- Convertible screened porch
- Two entries with air locks to deter winter drafts
- Bathroom and laundry located near shop for easy cleanup

- Kitchen with seating for up to ten
- Enhanced electrical system to provide power for shop equipment
- Workshop with garage-style doors for easy access

Laundry
(5' x 5')

up

Family room
(15' x 18' 6")

Fireplace

Dining area
(11' x 10' 6")

Bathroom
(7' 6" x 5')

Mud room
(12' 6" x 6')

Workshop
(13' x 19')

33' 6"

Kitchen
(11' x 8')

up

Covered porch

Foyer
(9' x 6')

Covered porch

56' 6"

The bell-curved roof

is a French import that adds a whimsical flair to an otherwise basic structure. You can experiment with siding methods and colors. Autumn reds, lime greens, and ivory are natural influences that have been a cheerful part of the French-Canadian heritage.

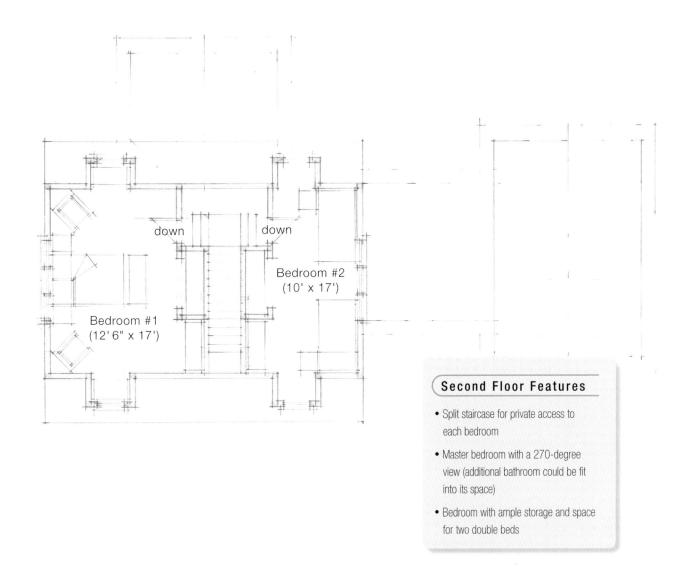

down   down

Bedroom #2
(10' x 17')

Bedroom #1
(12' 6" x 17')

Second Floor Features

- Split staircase for private access to each bedroom

- Master bedroom with a 270-degree view (additional bathroom could be fit into its space)

- Bedroom with ample storage and space for two double beds

A well-crafted small structure can have tremendous impact. This 750-square-foot cottage is appealing and practical by any standards.

The screened porch is 8 feet in depth, the same as the porch on the Settlement House. It is the minimum workable size that I recommend.

▲ This building is stripped for a major renovation.

The charm of old cottages leads us to put up with some unpleasant conditions and states of disrepair we would not even consider in our regular homes. I read once about a local cottage where a beaver kept chewing through the front door and taking up residence . . . while the owners were there! Even with the ensuing damage neither owner nor guest was willing to leave, and they managed to find a balance that worked for both of them.

But eventually, many people will end up considering a major renovation or restoration of an existing property. Why renovate? There may be a number of good reasons. Your cottage may have irreplaceable value as part of your family heritage. You may not be able to easily reconstruct in the same scenic location. The millwork and finishing detail in an historical structure may be too costly to replace today.

As passionate as you may be about your property, not all renovations are viable. The end product must provide spaces that are practical and attractive. Renovations can be even more expensive than new construction. Sometimes the structure is so badly deteriorated it doesn't make any financial sense to repair it. The state of the foundation and framing and the amount of rot and pest damage are the most significant factors to evaluate. After filling out this checklist, you may want to take your results to local building authorities and contractors.

▶ General Overview

Stand back and take a look at the exterior of your cottage.

- Are there signs of settling?
- Are there obvious signs of rot?
- Are there signs of carpenter ants or termites?
- How is the drainage around the structure?

▶ Exterior Foundation and Basement Walls

Cottages are often built on rock, steep slopes, or unstable soils.

- **Sonotubes:** Are they straight, and are major framing members still anchored properly?
- **Block piers:** Are they shifting? Is the foundation still anchored appropriately?
- **Full foundation:** Is there any severe cracking? Do the foundation walls lean? Are the joints sound? Are they collecting water?

▶ Exterior Walls

Most problems are caused by moisture, poor maintenance, and insect damage.

- Is wood siding still intact? Is it twisted, rotted, or infested with insects?
- Are the window frames decayed?
- Is the masonry intact, including chimneys?
- What is the condition of decks and exterior millwork?

▲ Check masonry for cracks; most can be easily be repaired.

▶ Roofs

Roofs should be checked when they are dry.

• Are there visible signs of worn or missing shingles?

• Are troughs in the eaves and all flashings still intact?

• Are there visible signs of leaking on exterior or interior walls?

• Is there adequate ventilation in the roof and soffit?

▶ Doors and Windows

• Are doors and windows functioning properly?

• Do they still have adequate weather seals?

• Do locking mechanisms still work?

• Are there enough windows and doors to meet practical and safety requirements?

▶ Interior Rooms

• Is the structure insulated appropriately for your recreational needs?

• What is the condition of walls, trim, and doors?

• Are all mechanical systems safe and appropriate to your requirements?

• Are all electrical systems safe and appropriate to your requirements?

• Are all plumbing systems safe and appropriate to your requirements?

• What is the condition of the flooring?

▶ Millwork/Cabinetwork

• What is the general condition of all kitchen, bathroom, and built-in cabinetwork?

• Are stairways safe and conveniently placed?

• Are railings safe and intact?

▶ Fireplaces

• Does the fireplace draw properly?

• Does it meet your heating requirements, or is it a heat loss factor?

• Has the unit been cleaned and inspected top to bottom recently?

▶ Storage

• Are general storage requirements met?

• Are mechanical/electrical services housed in a contained, warm, and dry area?

• Do you have storage for recreational items such as sporting goods and small water vessels?

▲ Exposed wood is susceptible to rot.

▲ Roofs and hard-to-reach trimwork are often poorly maintained.

▲ Bugs and rodents can leave extensive damage behind.

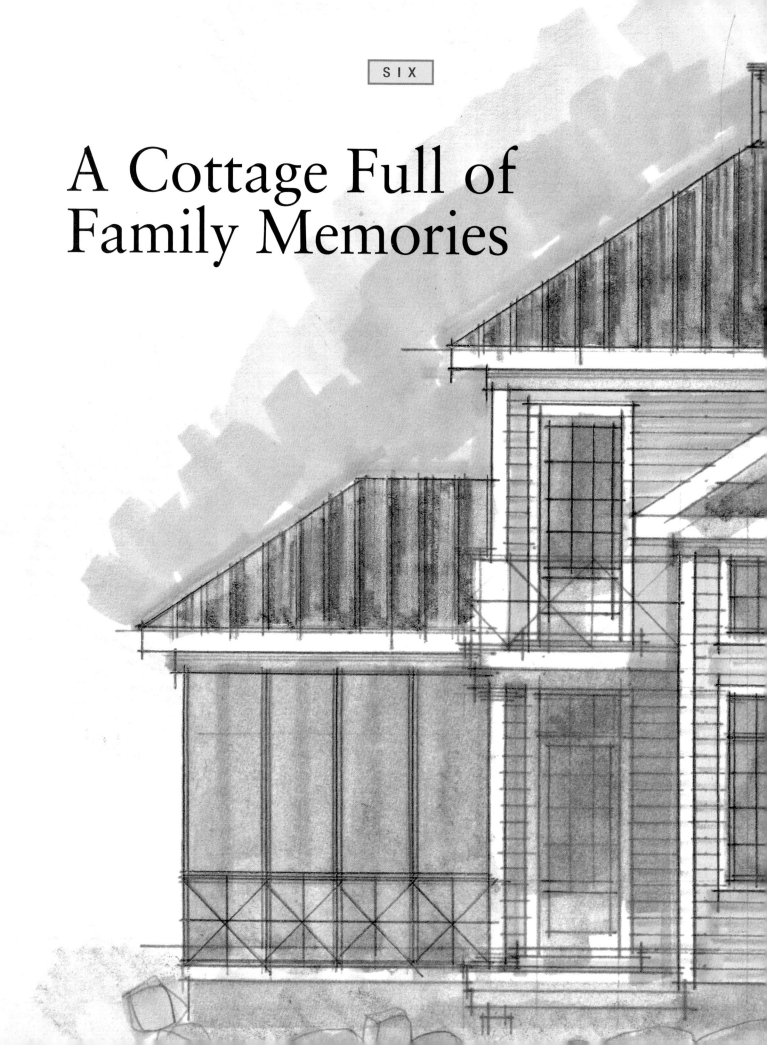

SIX

A Cottage Full of Family Memories

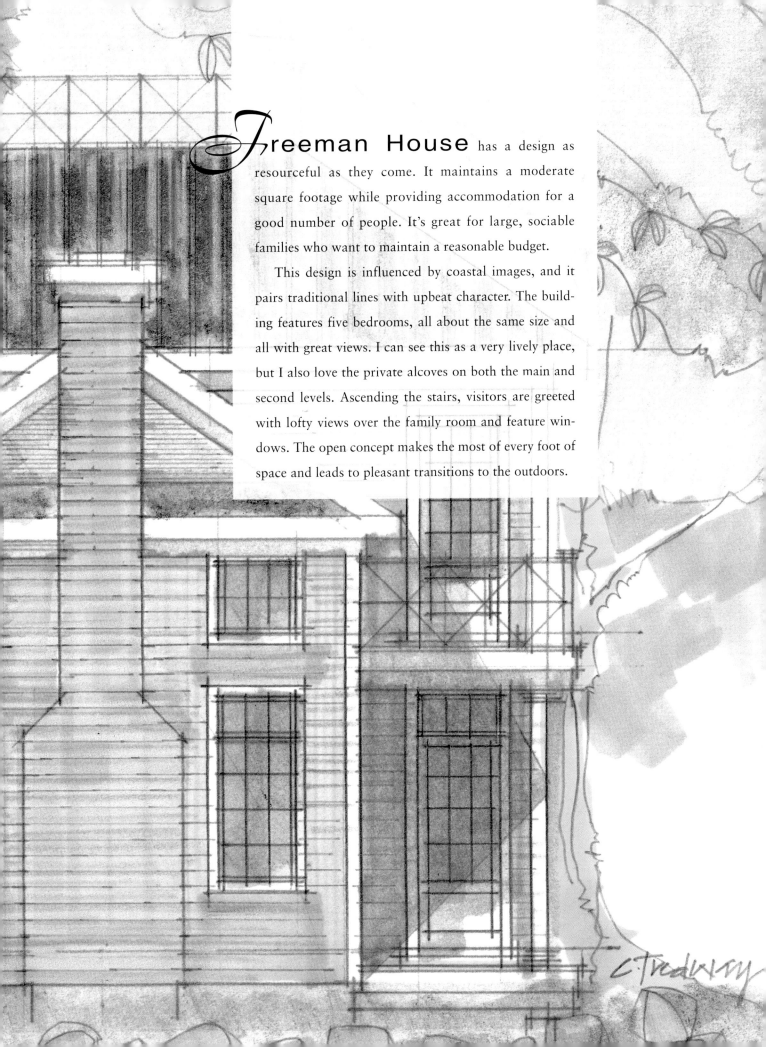

𝓕reeman House has a design as resourceful as they come. It maintains a moderate square footage while providing accommodation for a good number of people. It's great for large, sociable families who want to maintain a reasonable budget.

This design is influenced by coastal images, and it pairs traditional lines with upbeat character. The building features five bedrooms, all about the same size and all with great views. I can see this as a very lively place, but I also love the private alcoves on both the main and second levels. Ascending the stairs, visitors are greeted with lofty views over the family room and feature windows. The open concept makes the most of every foot of space and leads to pleasant transitions to the outdoors.

Building Style	Coastal
Bedrooms	5
Bathrooms	2
First Floor Area	872 sq. ft.
Second Floor Area	584 sq. ft.
Total Floor Area	1,456 sq. ft.

Front Elevation Features

- Impressive front entry with decorative glazing and tall columns

- Decorative railing at roof peak and on porches

- Screened porch

Right Elevation Features

- View of decorative windows in family room

- Screened porch with bold columns

- Balconies at first and second levels

A simple change in finishes can completely change a cottage's style. Freeman House reflects the vibrant coastal architecture style of the south. The photos shown here are of Georgian details from cottages in Rockport, Massachusetts. You can apply these features to the basic design of the Freeman House to create a very different look.

▲ An iron rail makes for a formal addition.

▲ A recessed front entry with decorative surround is a simple modification that makes a big impact.

▲ Alternate shapes for windows add personal style.

▲ A gently detailed entry provides a friendly welcome.

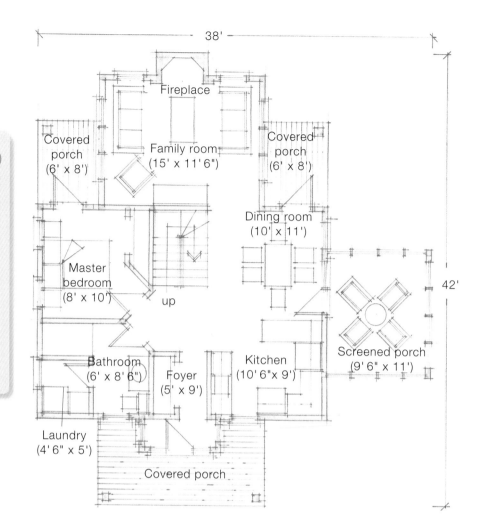

38'

42'

Fireplace

Covered porch
(6' x 8')

Family room
(15' x 11' 6")

Covered porch
(6' x 8')

Dining room
(10' x 11')

Master bedroom
(8' x 10')

up

Screened porch
(9' 6" x 11')

Bathroom
(6' x 8' 6")

Foyer
(5' x 9')

Kitchen
(10' 6"x 9')

Laundry
(4' 6" x 5')

Covered porch

First Floor Features

- Three covered porches
- Screened porch offers an alternative living space
- Open concept kitchen
- Master bedroom with adjacent bathroom suite
- Laundry room
- Staircase with balcony overlooking family room and feature windows
- Family room with cathedral ceiling

▲ A coach lamp, found in a variety of finishes across North America.

The position and style of lighting should be considered early in the design process. Other electrical requirements may become more evident during the construction process, as future cottage residents gain a better idea of likely room layouts and their particular needs for outlets and appliances. Lighting, on the other hand, is something I consider carefully and that I suggest the client think about right from the start.

Both interior and exterior lighting are key in creating a mood, highlighting points of interest, illuminating tasks and activities, and ensuring safety. Outside the cottage, watch for points of entry and for interesting landscape and architectural features that merit special attention. Safety lighting should be placed discreetly but functionally. Many standard fixtures now come equipped with motion-sensing devices.

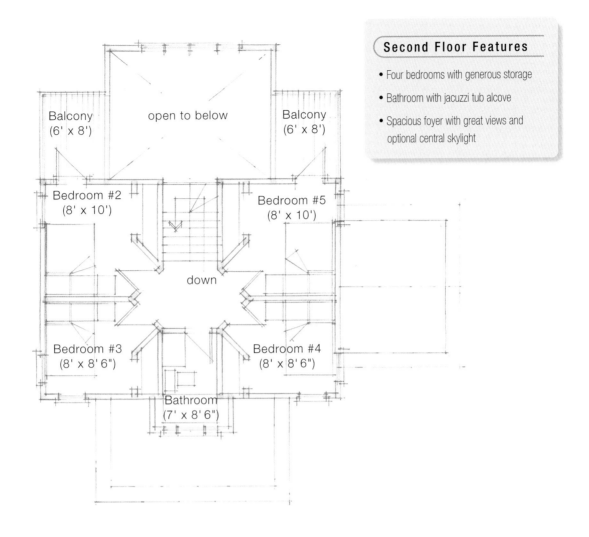

Balcony
(6' x 8')

open to below

Balcony
(6' x 8')

Bedroom #2
(8' x 10')

Bedroom #5
(8' x 10')

down

Bedroom #3
(8' x 8' 6")

Bedroom #4
(8' x 8' 6")

Bathroom
(7' x 8' 6")

Second Floor Features

- Four bedrooms with generous storage
- Bathroom with jacuzzi tub alcove
- Spacious foyer with great views and optional central skylight

▲ A good choice in lighting fixtures can make an entryway a dramatic focal point.

▲ Art lighting found at a desert site.

SEVEN

Cozy Cottage in Key West

$\mathcal{T}$he Truman House was first inspired ten years ago when I was designing a series of cottages for a Bermuda development. Over the years various versions of this plan have sparked the interest of clients from all parts of North America. Full access front and rear, a bungalow styling, and open living areas make the cottage fit right into most landscapes. For a small building it has an interesting and functional layout.

In any project, my goal is to develop a plan to meet the cultural, personal, and financial requirements of the client. The same floor plan can have many different outcomes in the elevations. With this plan I've provided two alternate possible elevations on the following page.

Building Style	Varies by elevation
Bedrooms	2
Bathrooms	1
Total Floor Area	801 sq. ft.

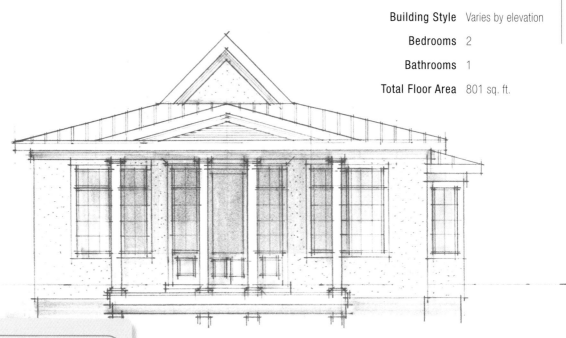

Front Elevation Features, Alternative "A"

- Palladian-style front porch
- Hip-style metal roof
- Nine-foot ceiling on main floor
- Generous glazing with transom windows

Front Elevation Features, Alternative "B"

- Lookout tower from second-floor loft
- Coastal detailing
- Square columns on optional screened porch
- Clapboard or stucco siding

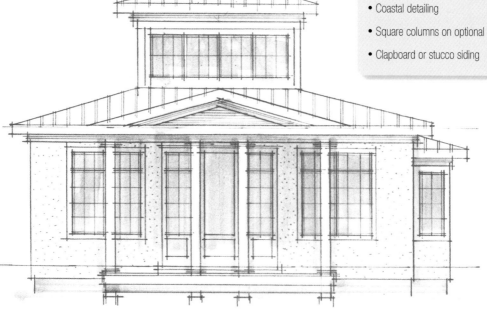

▲ Colors of the nearby ocean can inspire a palette for building exteriors.

▲ Fine railing details and a tongue-and-groove wood ceiling provide finishing touches.

▲ Full front porches are decorative and inviting.

▲ Landscape plantings and hard finishes can also give color cues for building exteriors.

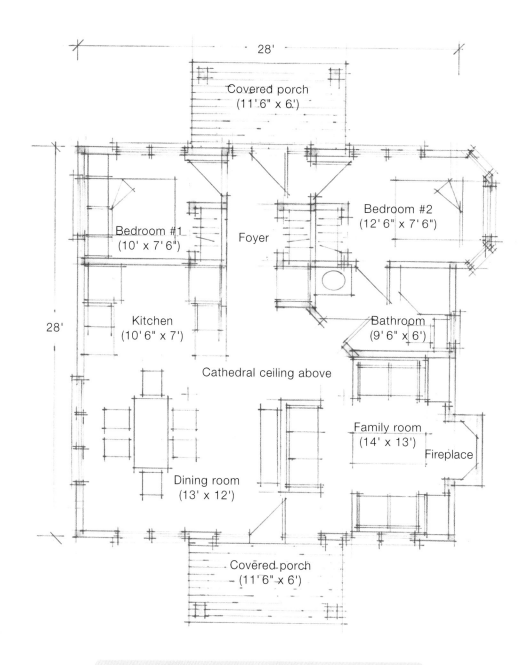

28'

Covered porch
(11'6" x 6')

Bedroom #1
(10' x 7'6")

Foyer

Bedroom #2
(12'6" x 7'6")

28'

Kitchen
(10'6" x 7')

Bathroom
(9'6" x 6')

Cathedral ceiling above

Family room
(14' x 13')

Fireplace

Dining room
(13' x 12')

Covered porch
(11'6" x 6')

Floor Plan Features

- Covered entry porch
- Two bedrooms with standard closets and generous glazing
- Bedroom #2 features optional en suite attachment and bay nook for bed
- Foyer with closet and stacking laundry

- Open-concept living areas with fireplace in view throughout
- Full front glazing with the option of decking or a covered or screened porch
- Cathedral ceiling throughout

Outdoor art can be incorporated into the exterior of your cottage. There are really no rules that must be followed here; it's just whatever moves you. Some practical considerations might include:

- Color choices that complement the architecture
- Themes that reflect the culture of the area
- Textures that define the surroundings
- A scale appropriate to the structure
- Your personal taste and style

▲ A signature piece can help identify your cottage.

▲ Accenting with a regional work, such as this southwestern piece, is popular.

◀ Decorative dinner bells give life to a cottage.

EIGHT

Gourmet Cook's Getaway

𝒯he **Granite House** makes the most of some of my all-time favorite features: Second Empire style in a small country format, stone facing, and classic porch detailing. I am an avid cook but, like many people with busy work schedules, I find that spending a leisurely hour or two in the kitchen in my regular home is a rare luxury. I see a refuge such as this cottage as a place for great food, wine, and fun.

The mansard roof presents a variety of options in finishing materials. Slate and cedar are the most common finishes and are often applied with delicate patterning. The shape of the roof also maximizes the second-floor space with quaint dormer alcoves and a full-height ceiling throughout.

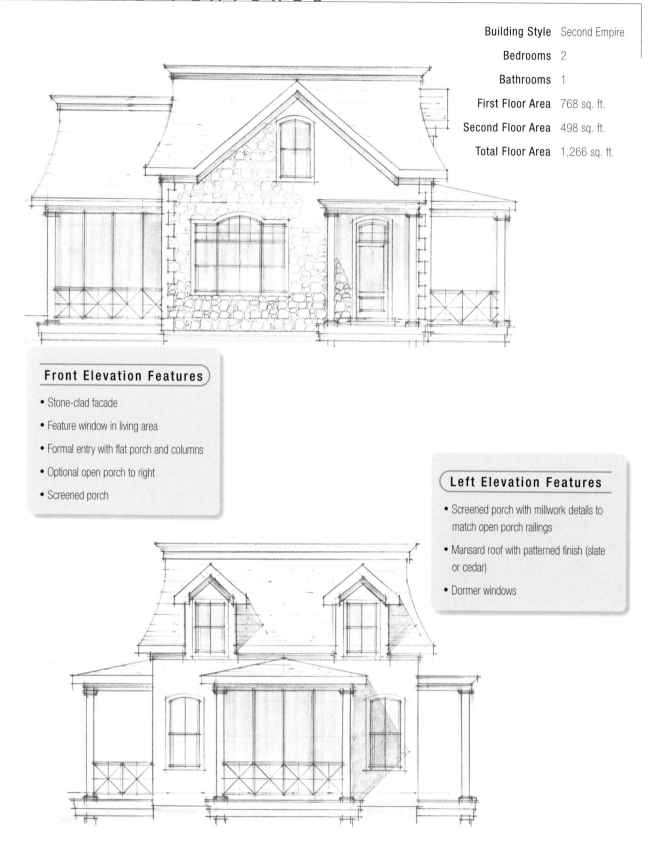

Building Style	Second Empire
Bedrooms	2
Bathrooms	1
First Floor Area	768 sq. ft.
Second Floor Area	498 sq. ft.
Total Floor Area	1,266 sq. ft.

Front Elevation Features

- Stone-clad facade
- Feature window in living area
- Formal entry with flat porch and columns
- Optional open porch to right
- Screened porch

Left Elevation Features

- Screened porch with millwork details to match open porch railings
- Mansard roof with patterned finish (slate or cedar)
- Dormer windows

Roofing should be durable and provide for local weather conditions. Consider the following when choosing your products:

• Cost (preparation and finish)
• Durability and longevity
• Building code requirements
• Color, texture, and pattern
• Compatibility of style with that of cottage
• Weather resistance
• Fire rating

In particular, remember that the roof's finish weight, depending on its slope, will be a significant load on the cottage's structure. In areas that receive snow, you must consider the maximum load during the snowiest winter. In regions prone to tornadoes and hurricanes, adhesion methods and resistance to wind shear are important. Here are some common roofing products to consider:

▶ **Asphalt and Fiberglass.**
Made of asphalt-impregnated organic felts coated with a layer of colored stone or ceramic gravel for color and texture.

▶ **Wood Shingles and Shakes.** Normally red cedar, white cedar, pine, redwood, or cypress; these types of shingles are characterized by fine grain, low expansion, low moisture, and natural water and insect resistance.

▲ Asphalt shingles come in various colors and profiles. (Check warranty periods, as they vary.)

▶ **Slate and Tile.** Slate is a natural stone that can last up to 100 years. Individual pieces may be susceptible to breakage from falling tree limbs.

▶ **Metal.** Made of aluminum, steel, or copper and available in shingle form, flat sheets, or panels. Metal is often formed and colored to reproduce other roofing finishes.

▲ Metal roofing comes in enameled, copper, and untreated finishes.

▶ **Roll Roofing.** Fiberglass-based roll roofing is used in low slope or flat applications (single layer underlay for low slope, double layer for flat). In all applications drainage is a key consideration.

▶ **Alternatives.** Clay tile, thatch or reed, composite wood, and plastic are emerging as more popular finishes. Review local climate and code conditions to see which may be suitable for your site.

▲ Cedar shingle roofing has an attractive, natural look and will generally last fifty years when properly applied.

▲ Alternative roofing products such as thatch, clay tile, and man-made reproductions create a distinctive historic look.

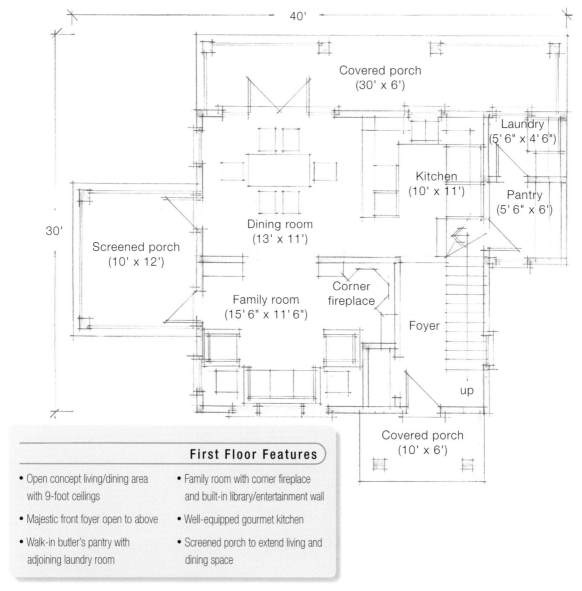

Covered porch
(30' x 6')

Laundry
(5' 6" x 4' 6")

Kitchen
(10' x 11')

Pantry
(5' 6" x 6')

40'

30'

Screened porch
(10' x 12')

Dining room
(13' x 11')

Corner
fireplace

Family room
(15' 6" x 11' 6")

Foyer

up

Covered porch
(10' x 6')

First Floor Features

- Open concept living/dining area with 9-foot ceilings

- Majestic front foyer open to above

- Walk-in butler's pantry with adjoining laundry room

- Family room with corner fireplace and built-in library/entertainment wall

- Well-equipped gourmet kitchen

- Screened porch to extend living and dining space

Using natural building materials always creates an interesting palette of color and texture. The mansard roof in the cottage shown here is an opportunity for a creative roofing application. Slate is laid with level or angled courses and multiple color combinations.

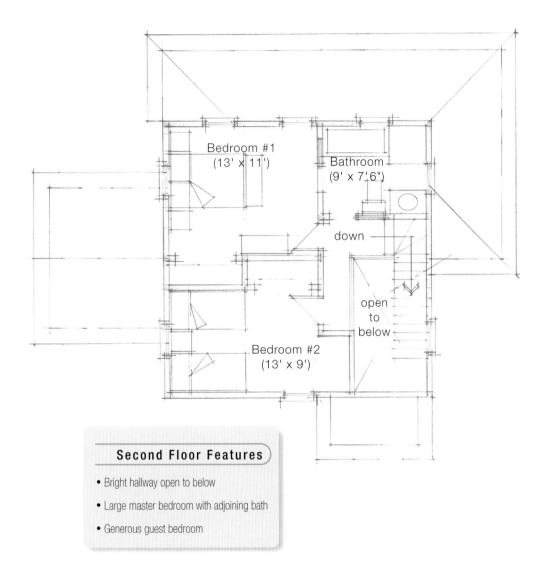

Bedroom #1
(13' x 11')

Bathroom
(9' x 7'6")

down

open
to
below

Bedroom #2
(13' x 9')

Second Floor Features

- Bright hallway open to below

- Large master bedroom with adjoining bath

- Generous guest bedroom

Stone products and their reproductions are available in all shapes and sizes. Note the decorative finial, blocks in contrasting color around the window, signage, and shingles, all created from stone in this classic cottage.

1892

ROCKPORT GRANITE CO.

NINE

Reader's Haven on the Coast

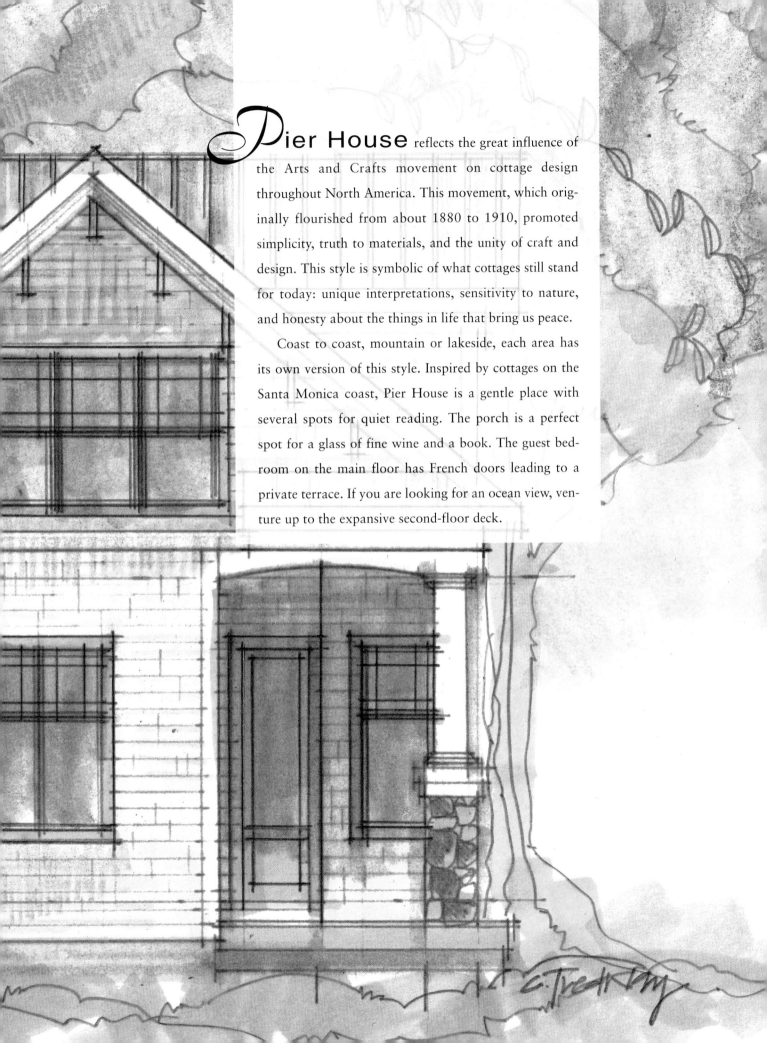

$\mathcal{P}$ier House reflects the great influence of the Arts and Crafts movement on cottage design throughout North America. This movement, which originally flourished from about 1880 to 1910, promoted simplicity, truth to materials, and the unity of craft and design. This style is symbolic of what cottages still stand for today: unique interpretations, sensitivity to nature, and honesty about the things in life that bring us peace.

Coast to coast, mountain or lakeside, each area has its own version of this style. Inspired by cottages on the Santa Monica coast, Pier House is a gentle place with several spots for quiet reading. The porch is a perfect spot for a glass of fine wine and a book. The guest bedroom on the main floor has French doors leading to a private terrace. If you are looking for an ocean view, venture up to the expansive second-floor deck.

Building Style   Craftsman

Bedrooms   2

Bathrooms   2

First Floor Area   776 sq. ft.

Second Floor Area   594 sq. ft.

Total Floor Area   1,370 sq. ft.

Rear Elevation Features

- Exposed rafters
- Cedar shingle siding
- Metal roofing
- Decorative window grill in double-hung window
- Large window grouping from master bedroom

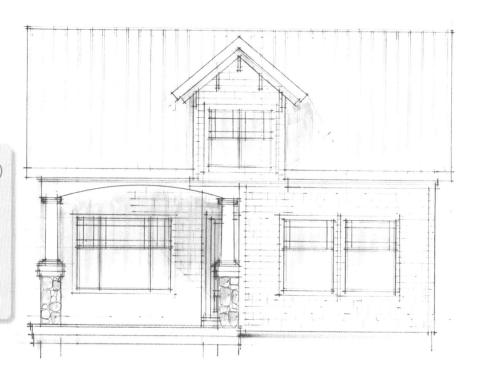

Right Elevation Features

- Covered porch with stone pillars to support columns
- Dormer window for second floor bathroom
- Picture window brings light into family room

The Arts and Crafts movement was a reaction to the poor-quality, mass-produced goods of the late 1800s. The simple, often unornamented style requires quality materials, fine craftsmanship, and sensitivity to the surrounding environment.

The Craftsman's cottage spread like wildfire throughout North America. Note the striking resemblance between the examples at top left (in Rockport, Massachusetts) and at bottom left (in Santa Monica, California).

Attention to detail is the key to the successful outcome of these designs. Windows are often embellished with decorative grill patterns. Soffits often have millwork cut with delicate patterns (below).

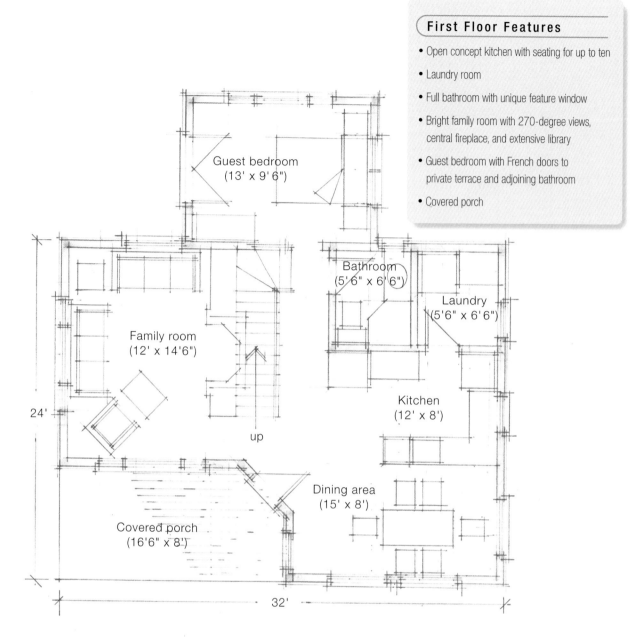

Guest bedroom
(13' x 9' 6")

Bathroom
(5' 6" x 6' 6")

Laundry
(5' 6" x 6' 6")

Family room
(12' x 14' 6")

Kitchen
(12' x 8')

up

Dining area
(15' x 8')

Covered porch
(16' 6" x 8')

24'

32'

Consider embellishing

your own building with unique details in keeping with tradition. Note how the fine "bell curve" provides a delicate novelty to the exterior wall. Take a driving tour and photograph the ideas that appeal to you!

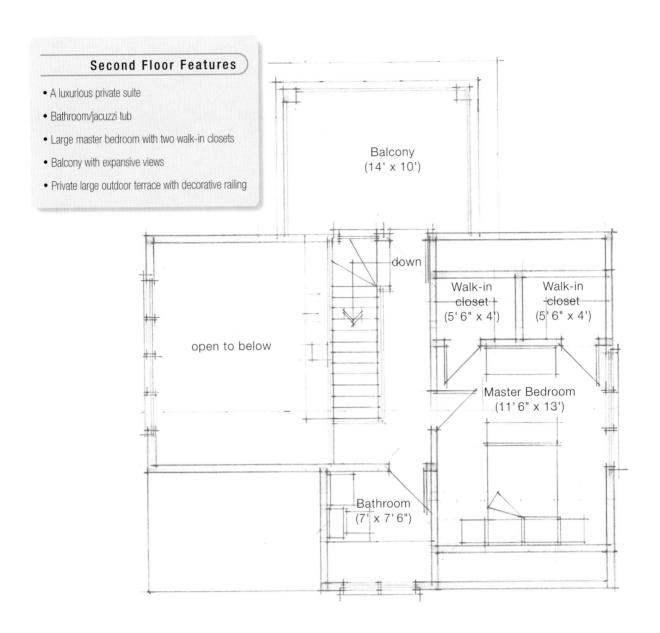

Second Floor Features

- A luxurious private suite
- Bathroom/jacuzzi tub
- Large master bedroom with two walk-in closets
- Balcony with expansive views
- Private large outdoor terrace with decorative railing

Balcony
(14' x 10')

open to below

down

Walk-in closet
(5' 6" x 4')

Walk-in closet
(5' 6" x 4')

Master Bedroom
(11' 6" x 13')

Bathroom
(7' x 7' 6")

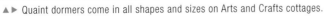
▲▶ Quaint dormers come in all shapes and sizes on Arts and Crafts cottages.

TEN

An Oasis in the Desert

$\mathcal{T}$aos Cottage is a result of a trip I took to New Mexico a few years ago. I was taken with the purity of adobe structures. The buildings I saw — all set against the fleshy local sand, turquoise sky, and local brown barks — embodied a perfect marriage between built and natural things. Besides that, I just love homes where the inside spills to the outside with lush garden terraces, colorful pottery, and textiles hanging out to air.

This design is inspired by the adobe method, but it could easily be built with more conventional materials. The cottage breaks down distinctions between indoors and out with its multiple French doors, its porches, and its private garden terrace. A fireplace or kiva forms the centerpiece of the open living/dining areas.

I envision high ceilings with round, rough-hewn logs stained white. Saltillo tiles and sisal rugs would cover the floor for an earthy finish.

GENERAL FEATURES

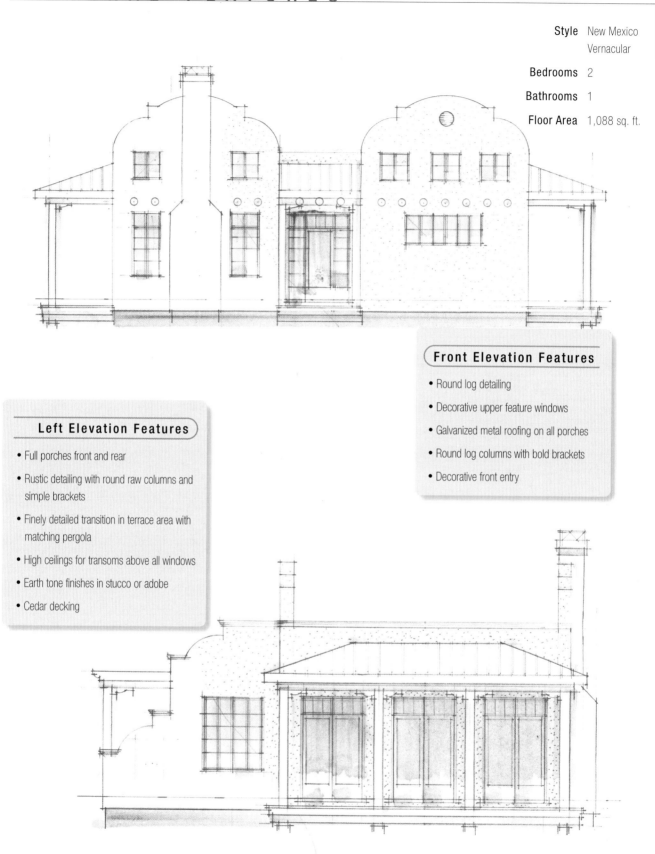

Style New Mexico
Vernacular

Bedrooms 2

Bathrooms 1

Floor Area 1,088 sq. ft.

Front Elevation Features

- Round log detailing

- Decorative upper feature windows

- Galvanized metal roofing on all porches

- Round log columns with bold brackets

- Decorative front entry

Left Elevation Features

- Full porches front and rear

- Rustic detailing with round raw columns and simple brackets

- Finely detailed transition in terrace area with matching pergola

- High ceilings for transoms above all windows

- Earth tone finishes in stucco or adobe

- Cedar decking

Traditional adobe designs have flat roofs and decorative gables oriented toward the street. Clay is the most common color (generated from local soils). Round logs protruding from the building face are structural members in true adobe construction but can be applied later when conventional methods are used.

The adobe structure is a perfect match for its natural landscape. I love the texture and ease of this lifestyle.

The post and bracket details (at left) are typically rustic and often left untreated. A suitable stain color is applied here for a complementary finish.

A common color combination in this part of New Mexico — the earthy tones of adobe walls against the deep blue of the sky — gives a clear inspiration for stain choices.

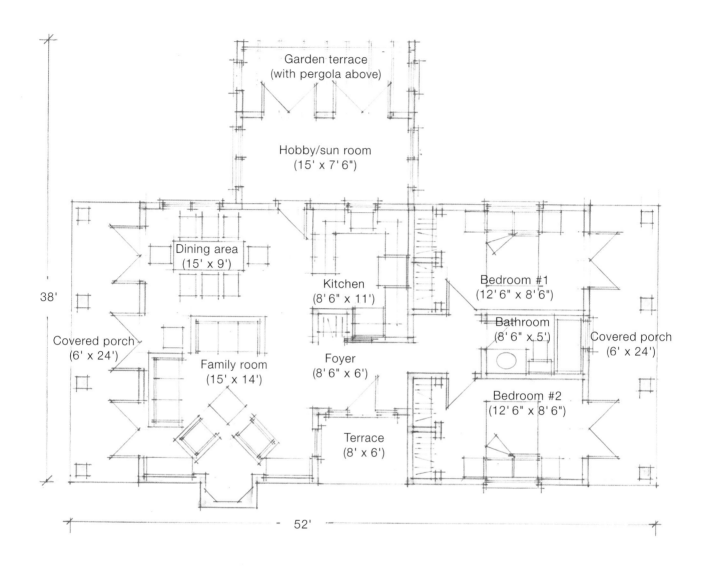

Garden terrace
(with pergola above)

Hobby/sun room
(15' x 7' 6")

38'

Dining area
(15' x 9')

Kitchen
(8' 6" x 11')

Bedroom #1
(12' 6" x 8' 6")

Covered porch
(6' x 24')

Bathroom
(8' 6" x 5')

Covered porch
(6' x 24')

Family room
(15' x 14')

Foyer
(8' 6" x 6')

Bedroom #2
(12' 6" x 8' 6")

Terrace
(8' x 6')

52'

First Floor Features

- Full-length covered porches front and rear
- French doors throughout
- A hobby/sun room with adjoining garden terrace and arbor
- Kiva stove
- Bedrooms have awning windows and private doors to porch
- Generous storage throughout

Authentic and creative details can turn an ordinary cottage into one that seems utterly natural yet full of pleasant surprises.

The planters and their gracefully curving lights at left seem to grow naturally out of the adobe wall. Natural elements like this bring life to a cottage.

In a dry climate, this fountain's combination of cool water splashing against warm stone makes a big impact.

In any cottage setting, water is an element to consider adding. It is restful to look at, listen to, or just dip one's hand in.

This fence detail at near right incorporates masonry methods with natural posts. The lengths of wood between the pillars are a great example of indigenous materials used to add a sense of belonging. Note how these wooden posts blend into the slender trunks of the trees behind them.

At far right, colorful doors make for enticing gateways to interior courtyards.

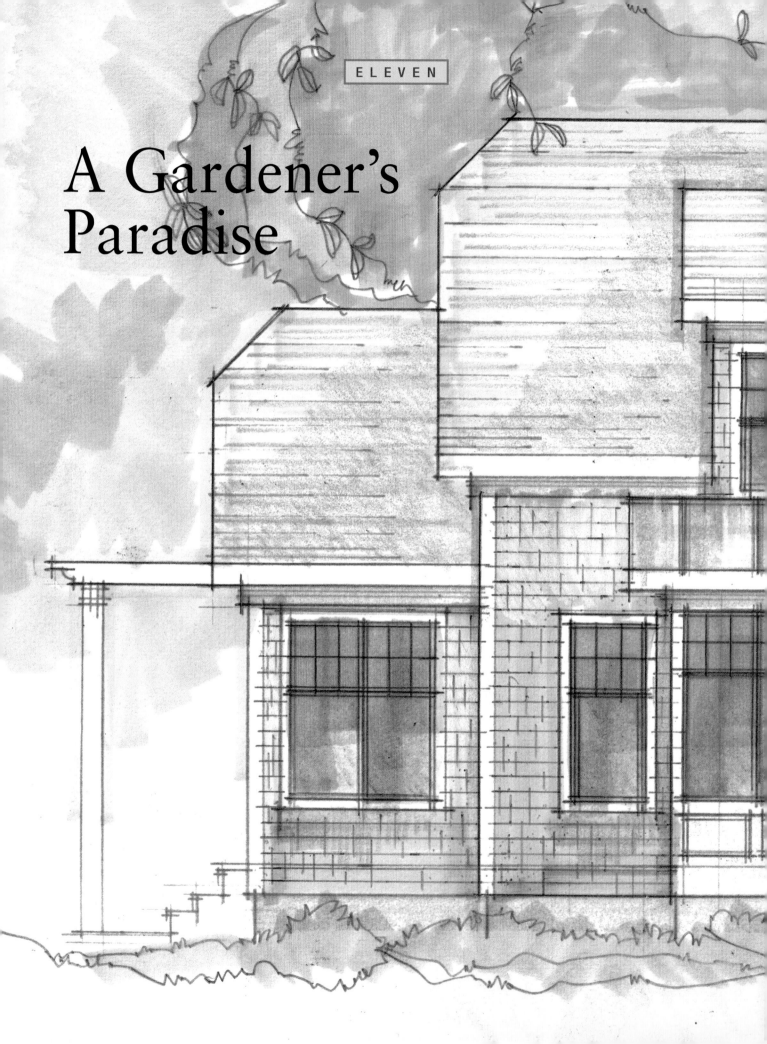

ELEVEN

A Gardener's Paradise

The Shaw House is sure to be a treasured sanctuary for the garden or hobby enthusiast. To me, its styling is old England meets Cape Cod. Open vistas allow for 360-degree views while you are nestled in your own flowering Eden. A whitewashed shingle exterior and a colorful metal roof serve as the blank canvas for your gardening brushstrokes. A pergola and an interior potting shed bring the outside in, and the screened porch has full millwork detail and panoramic windows. One might consider a whitewashed finish with timber detailing for the open, casual interior. A cathedral ceiling over the living room provides a feeling of spaciousness to a relatively compact plan. With bedrooms on both the first and second floors, the Shaw House is a design suited to young or old.

Building Style	Cape Cod	**First Floor Area**	1,071 sq. ft.
Bedrooms	3	**Second Floor Area**	552 sq. ft
Bathrooms	2	**Total Floor Area**	1,623 sq. ft.

Front Elevation Features

- Pergola with stone terrace for outdoor living area
- Screened porch
- Potting area next to pergola
- Stucco and vertical siding
- Attention to detail in trim of windows and porches
- Dutch roof

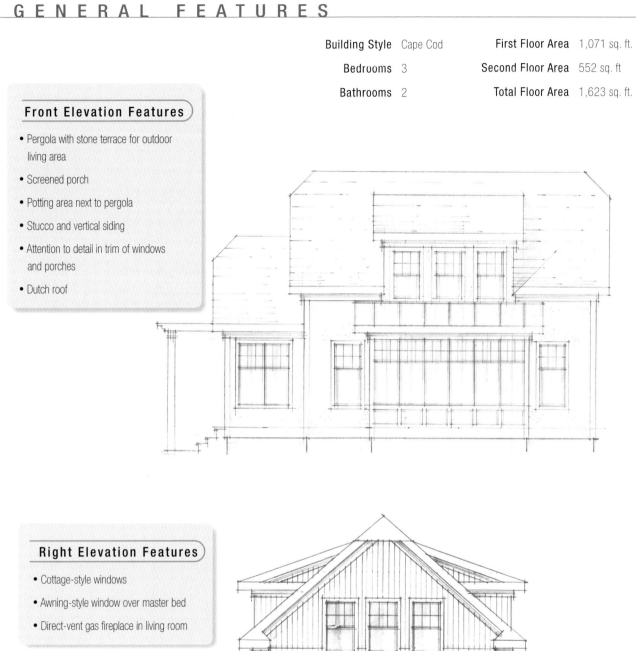

Right Elevation Features

- Cottage-style windows
- Awning-style window over master bed
- Direct-vent gas fireplace in living room

The Dutch-style roof features in the Shaw House make for a North American version of the traditional English cottage roof. These roofs are characteristically high pitched and provide for a quaint appearance.

Note the expanse of exposed roof in these samples. I would recommend having some fun with this feature; consider colored metal, colored high-quality asphalt, cedar, or even slate for this application.

Alternatives you might consider for siding include cedar shingles, vertical siding and stucco, or an upbeat white-washed version of the English timber house.

This style of roof is a good example of a transformation of a traditional form. Originally, roofs like this may have been constructed of thatch and with walls of stone. These modern versions demonstrate how cottages can preserve subtle hints of the past.

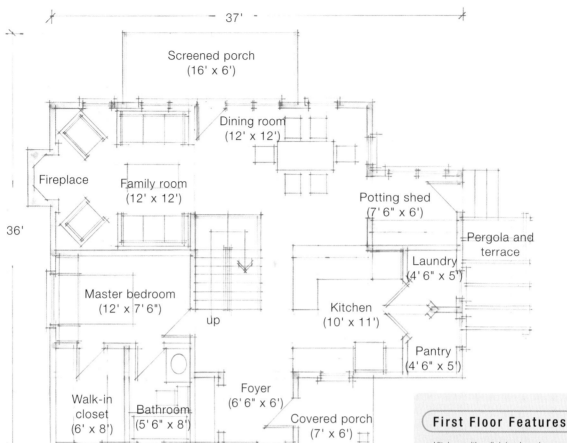

- 37' -

Screened porch
(16' x 6')

Dining room
(12' x 12')

Fireplace

Family room
(12' x 12')

Potting shed
(7' 6" x 6')

Pergola and
terrace

36'

Laundry
(4' 6" x 5')

Master bedroom
(12' x 7' 6")

up

Kitchen
(10' x 11')

Pantry
(4' 6" x 5')

Walk-in
closet
(6' x 8')

Bathroom
(5' 6" x 8')

Foyer
(6' 6" x 6')

Covered porch
(7' x 6')

The garden details

such as a pergola and potting shed applied to this plan could be completely changed, depending on your hobby. A photographer might substitute a dark room and a glass gallery; a painter might need an art supply storage/sink station and a glass studio. The possibilities are endless.

In the gardener's case, I have recommended a white background for the potential sea of color. You may also want to consider your favorite plants when choosing an exterior palette. How about butter yellow with moss and white trim, or silver gray with ivory and maroon trim? Think of designing and painting the cottage as the first step in your garden design.

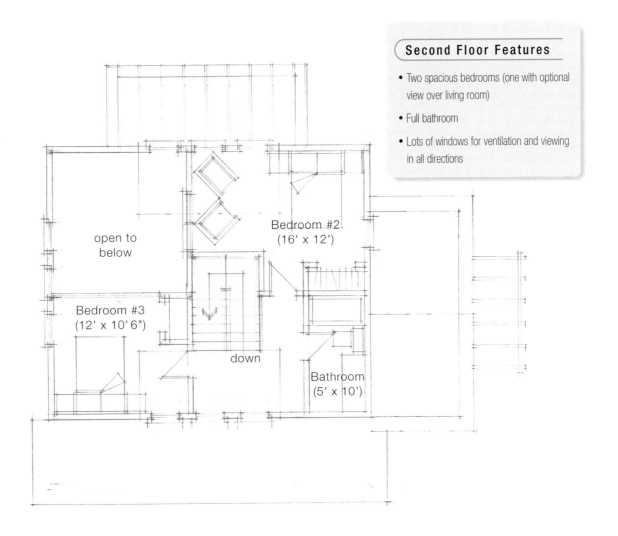

open to below

Bedroom #2 (16' x 12')

Bedroom #3 (12' x 10' 6")

down

Bathroom (5' x 10')

These window boxes give examples of the vibrant color combinations your garden cottage can serve as a backdrop for.

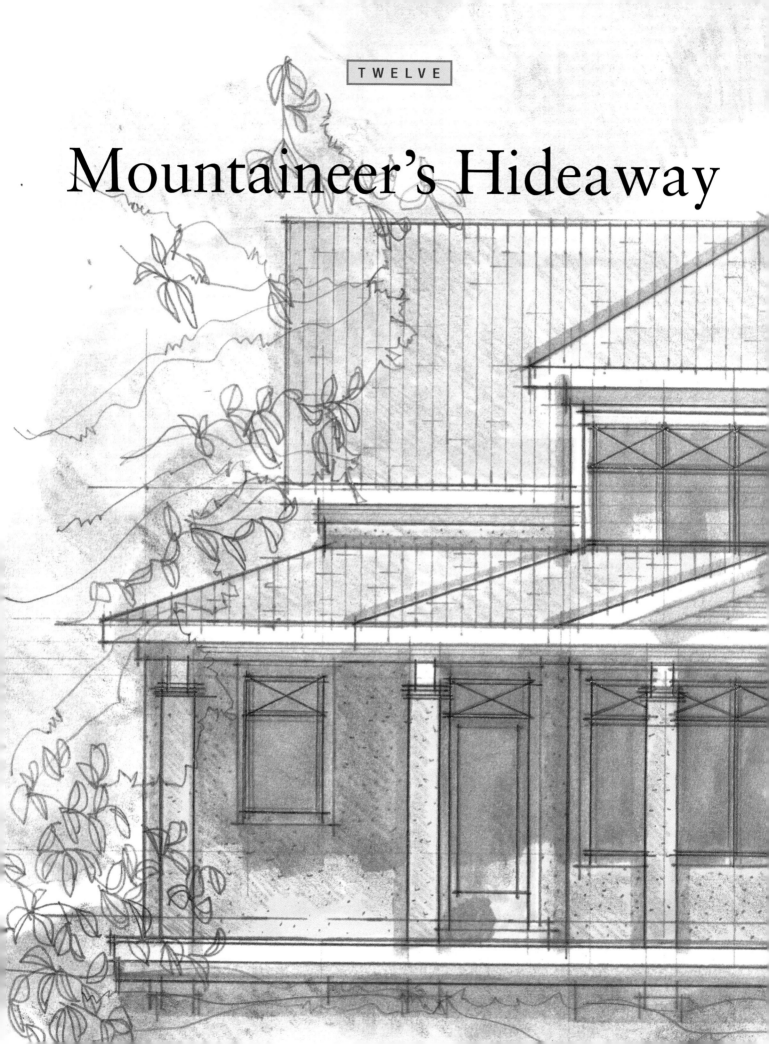

TWELVE

Mountaineer's Hideaway

The Sundance is a place for casual, outdoor living. On a visit to Utah I was greatly impressed by great diversity of the landscape: vast, rocky desert to the south, not far from breathtaking mountain terrain. What influenced me most there was the fresh air. Water cascades, lakes, red rock — I knew that any cottage I designed there must be a continuation of what was happening outside.

Expansive wraparound porches allow you to follow the land wherever it may take you. There is southwestern stucco styling, contemporary posting, and fresh grill patterns. The entertainment room features a kiva-style fireplace and built-ins for a library or home theater, and living areas extend from the kitchen to form a great room. I see the Sundance perched on a mountain or beside a trickling stream. It's the perfect getaway for fly fisherman, rancher, and mountaineer alike.

GENERAL FEATURES

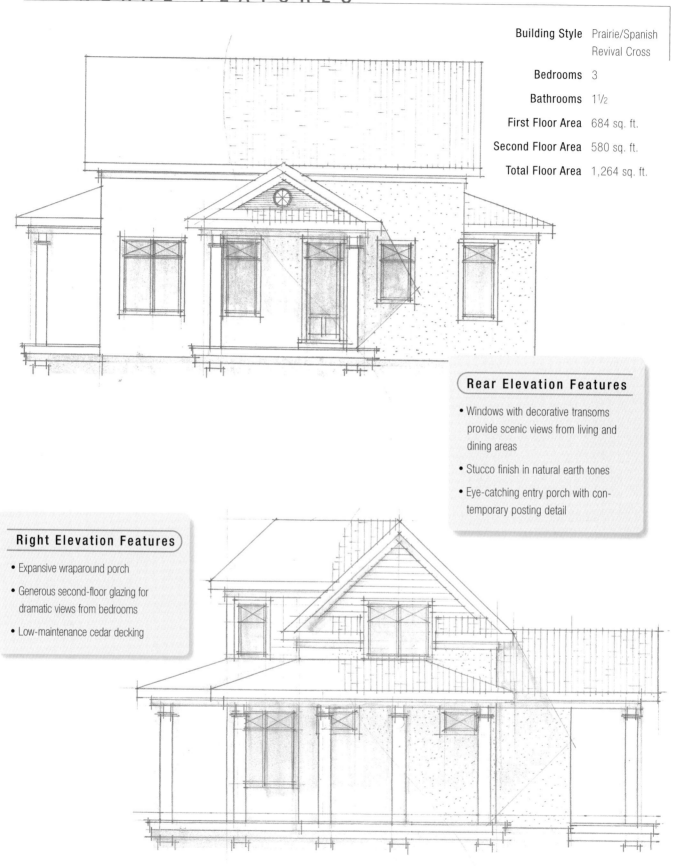

Building Style Prairie/Spanish Revival Cross

Bedrooms 3

Bathrooms 1½

First Floor Area 684 sq. ft.

Second Floor Area 580 sq. ft.

Total Floor Area 1,264 sq. ft.

Rear Elevation Features

- Windows with decorative transoms provide scenic views from living and dining areas

- Stucco finish in natural earth tones

- Eye-catching entry porch with contemporary posting detail

Right Elevation Features

- Expansive wraparound porch

- Generous second-floor glazing for dramatic views from bedrooms

- Low-maintenance cedar decking

Kivas and clay products of all types provide excellent accents for southwestern cottages (left). Kivas were originally round ceremonial structures in Pueblo Indian dewellings. Now they are often seen as adobe-style fireplaces, as would be used in the Sundance.

Banding and reveal details can be added for extra interest and a streak of color on the building facade (middle left). Carrying a contrasting color such as this throughout a building ties a design together.

Contemporary posting is an interesting alternative to more conventional millwork (middle right). Stucco columns can be capped with metal or clay details, or even complemented with local stone facing.

Desert and mountain influences aided in the development of the Sundance. The wildlife, vegetation, and natural coloration of the surrounding environment inspired color choices of taupe, charcoal, silver, and rust.

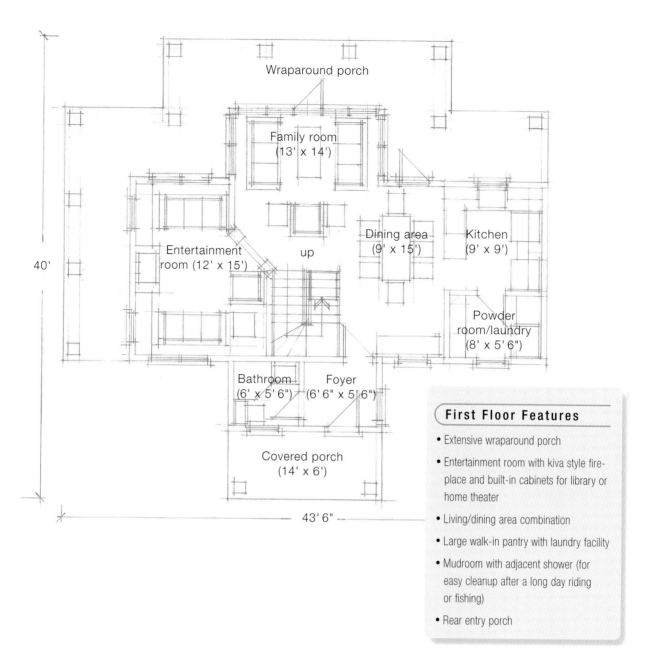

Wraparound porch

Family room
(13' x 14')

40'

Entertainment
room (12' x 15')

up

Dining area
(9' x 15')

Kitchen
(9' x 9')

Powder
room/laundry
(8' x 5'6")

Bathroom
(6' x 5'6")

Foyer
(6'6" x 5'6")

Covered porch
(14' x 6')

43'6"

Open rafters are seeing a reincarnation in all North American building climates. Originally these rafters were just an unfinished extension of the roof framing system. Carpenters occasionally went to the trouble of shaping the ends for a resourcefully appealing finish. By most standards this is an incomplete framing method, but certainly appropriate for a small summer cottage.

Today people often associate cottages with this endearing open rafter frame and go to great lengths and expense to recreate the look in a way that will meet modern insulation standards. In warmer climates this is still a common and permissible framing method.

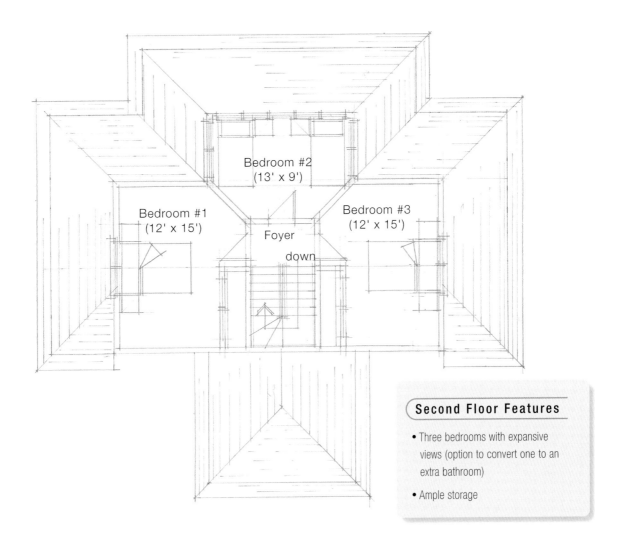

Bedroom #2
(13' x 9')

Bedroom #1
(12' x 15')

Bedroom #3
(12' x 15')

Foyer

down

Soffit is defined as the undersurface of any architectural feature, such as an arch, a lintel, a cornice, or a balcony. It is commonly constructed from wood, vinyl, or aluminum and can be vented or unvented. Soffit provides enclosure to framing members to deter nesting of bugs and birds.

A fascia provides the finishing touch to the ends of roof framing members. Structurally it helps to tie all of the pieces together.

Recreational properties have soffit and fascia in all varieties. Like the front door, the lofty soffit serves as a place for personal decorative touches.

▲ An Arts and Crafts motif has cleverly been cut into the fascia of this California cottage.

THIRTEEN

A Sport Enthusiast's Retreat

The Green Mountain House

recalls traditional North American barn styling with its simple lines, vertical siding, cupolas, and double-hung windows. It is suitable for either conventional or timber-frame construction, and the vaulted interior spaces are ideal for both casual and formal living. This cottage could be a weekend getaway or a regular retirement home; its style could fit into many types of recreational sites. Railings, millwork, and roofing provide opportunities for alternative finishes to personalize your property.

The interior plan has generous living spaces with a touch of luxury in the two private bedroom suites. The exercise room encourages a healthy lifestyle and complements a wholesome home. Additional sleeping areas could be built in a nearby bunkhouse.

c. tredway

Building Style	Colonial Revival
Bedrooms	2
Bathrooms	2½
First Floor Area	1,188 sq. ft.
Second Floor Area	558 sq. ft.
Total Floor Area	1,746 sq. ft.

Front Elevation Features

- Double dormers provide extra glazing for second-story bathroom and exercise area

- Covered entry is a strong central focus

- Potential for alternate millwork, posts, gable details, and glass designs

- Roof treatments could include metal, slate, asphalt, or cedar shingles

Rear Elevation Features

- Cupola is reminiscent of the traditional barn (could be open to below for an interesting alternative light source)

- Millwork detail of the feature window complements the screened porch

- Doors from the living and master bedroom areas provide direct access to decking

I have always loved this type of finely crafted mill-work detail (near right). It is more costly than conventional siding methods, but it can make quite an impact when applied to a relatively small area in a four-season porch.

Vertical wood siding in almost any style would be suitable for this design.

The front entry (left) is a particular strong focal point. Fine millwork, interesting doors, and stained glass inserts can all help to accentuate this feature. In this example the reclaimed wood door provides an authentically warm welcome.

A rustic approach can be cleverly accentuated with features such as "barn-style" shutters (above).

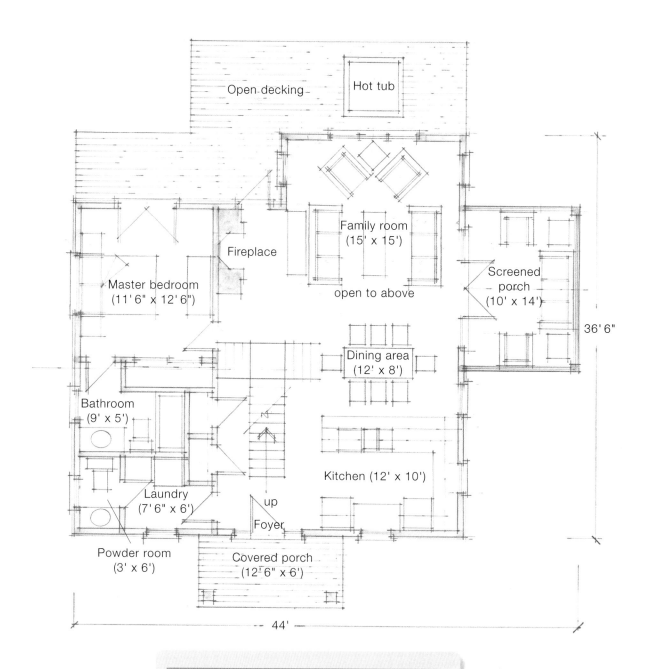

Open decking

Hot tub

Fireplace

Family room
(15' x 15')

open to above

Screened
porch
(10' x 14')

Master bedroom
(11' 6" x 12' 6")

Dining area
(12' x 8')

36' 6"

Bathroom
(9' x 5')

Kitchen (12' x 10')

Laundry
(7' 6" x 6')

up

Foyer

Powder room
(3' x 6')

Covered porch
(12' 6" x 6')

44'

First Floor Features

- Open concept living room with two-story fireplace (great for stone facing) and a large feature window

- Kitchen with view of surrounding environment

- Dining for up to twelve

- Screened porch extends living/dining spaces (could be converted to a year-round space)

- Private suite with bathroom/ jacuzzi and French doors to deck. Armoire for storage or entertainment unit

- Grand foyer with split-direction staircase and cathedral ceiling above; extra storage for coats

- Laundry room with adjacent powder room

- Quaint front porch for a friendly entry

- Bedroom suite #2 has private bath/jacuzzi, dormers, and balcony

- Exercise area with ample room for exercise gear and balcony overlooking main feature window

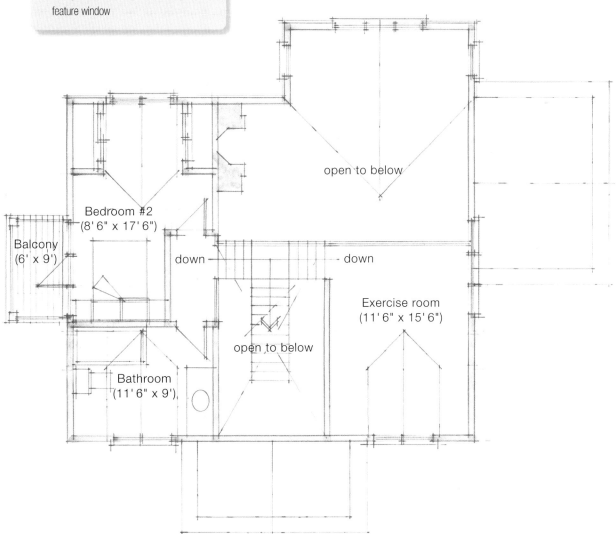

open to below

Bedroom #2
(8' 6" x 17' 6")

Balcony
(6' x 9')

down →

← down

Exercise room
(11' 6" x 15' 6")

open to below

Bathroom
(11' 6" x 9')

Choose siding according to climate, color, texture, and budget. Good design can maximize the visual appeal of the most basic finishes. The simple vertical siding of the Green Mountain House immediately identifies the origins of the design in traditional New England barns, such as the one below. The guest house pictured at left is an example of a high-quality vinyl siding combined with fine millwork details and an interesting roofline. Cedar shingles were stained to match the siding and are in the process of being installed.

Appropriate materials

are as important as good design. Wooden clapboards will add a classic touch to a range of traditional designs, and stone siding, such as that shown above, is a dramatic feature, both texturally and structurally.

Here are some basic guidelines to use when you are considering contractors to build your cottage:

- Anybody can get one good reference. **Ask to contact the clients of the last three projects.** Don't expect to hear that everything was perfect. Work on a reliable schedule, good communication skills, maturity, and responsible financial management are key.
- **Check out your contractors** with staff at local building yards. They are insiders who see contractor longevity, technical knowledge, and financial management firsthand. Word-of-mouth references are invaluable.
- **Consider all contractors who are qualified** for work. The recreational construction industry can be very booked-up at certain times, and local resources in your area can be quickly consumed. Slightly more distant contractors may be able to house themselves locally, provide better skills, and offer a more competitive price.
- On remote sites where you are unable to check in regularly, **hire an independent consultant to do periodic inspections.** The site contractor has the ultimate responsibility and should be respected accordingly, but a third party can verify whether the appropriate materials and construction methods are being used. Any irregularities should be photographed and documented to the contractor and owner immediately.
- **Provide a detailed set of specifications and a very specific contract.** Most owners focus on a cottage's design, but specifications are equally important. They define expectations clearly for both sides and help the job run smoothly. Even the best working relationships can be tainted by honest misunderstandings.
- **Work with your contractor on terms of payment** that work for both of you. I am a strong believer in a payment schedule that corresponds to the completion of various phases of construction. The idea is to keep the job on as even a keel as possible. Don't exclude a good contractor because he is unable to wait until the end of the project for payment.

  By the same token, large payments in advance are usually unwarranted and dangerous. A payment schedule that approximately meets payroll in two-week intervals should work for most contractors. Sometimes unforeseen circumstances, such as delays in deliveries of materials, will put the schedule out of order. Be prepared to make a few concessions during construction, but otherwise *do not deviate from your specifications or payment obligations.*

- I don't believe in strict deadlines, as I think this is a matter of mutual respect throughout the construction process. **Interview the contractor initially to make sure he has the resources to meet your expected deadline.** If the crew is not provided or performing as promised, it is grounds for terminating the contract. Assuming that all is going well, keep up your end of the bargain. On my projects I ask owners to provide payment within 48 hours after it is due. I recommend that contractors wait for each payment prior to proceeding.
- **Never proceed without a contract signed by both parties.** This is essential. Should you run into trouble, consult with a lawyer immediately. A draw payment schedule based on progress limits your exposure, but local laws will determine your overall contractual obligations.

  Changes from the contract should be documented, assigned a price, and authorized in writing throughout the construction. *Do not proceed unless this is done.* This is a trouble area for both contractors and owners. Contractors who do not document additional work often have difficulty collecting. Owners who do not document can have high cost overruns.

- **Make sure all inspections and permits are in order.** Do not issue final payment until all work is done and deficiencies are dealt with. Even the best-intentioned contractor gets tied up with the next job in line and finds returning difficult. I recommend that the contractor sign a "statutory declaration" indicating that all suppliers and tradespeople related to your project have been paid in full. Laws vary throughout North America, but most areas will hold the end user responsible for payment of all parties, regardless of advances to the general contractor. Check your local regulations.
- The construction of the cottage of your dreams won't turn into a nightmare as long as you remember to:
  1. Prepare well.
  2. Allow for unexpected and associated cost overruns (a minimum of 20 percent above your budget).
  3. Restrain yourself and stick to your budget whenever possible.
  4. Stick to your contract and document your construction.
  5. Keep positive lines of communication open with your contractor.
  6. Treat yourself and those around you well during the process. Then dream away!

FOURTEEN

Year-Round Haven for Hiking and Skiing

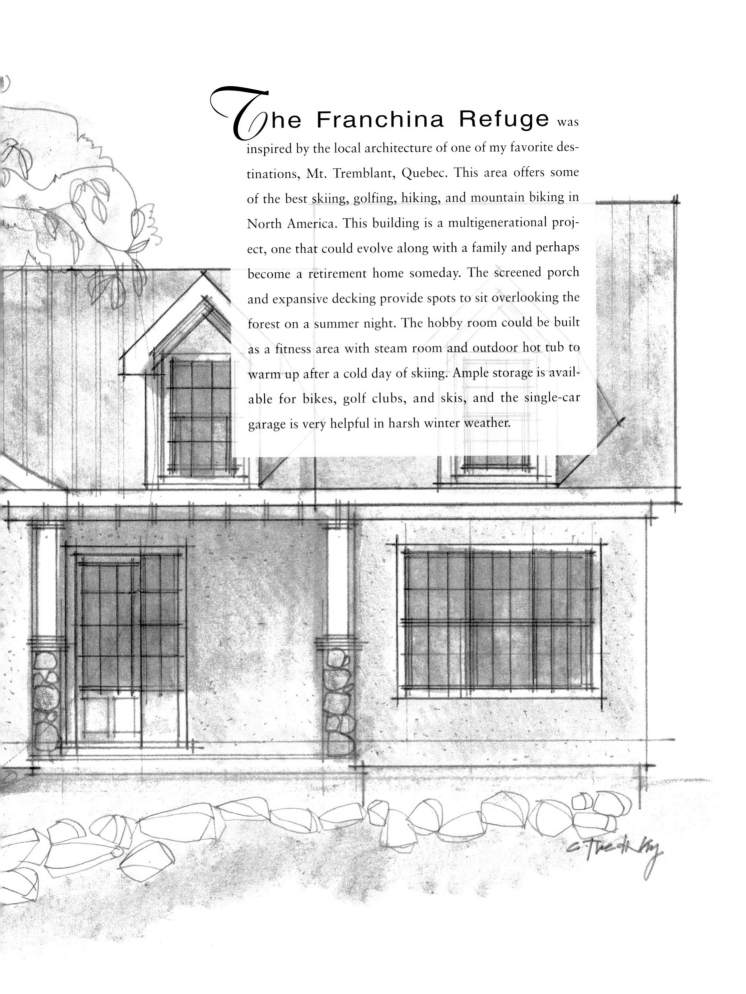

The Franchina Refuge was

inspired by the local architecture of one of my favorite destinations, Mt. Tremblant, Quebec. This area offers some of the best skiing, golfing, hiking, and mountain biking in North America. This building is a multigenerational project, one that could evolve along with a family and perhaps become a retirement home someday. The screened porch and expansive decking provide spots to sit overlooking the forest on a summer night. The hobby room could be built as a fitness area with steam room and outdoor hot tub to warm up after a cold day of skiing. Ample storage is available for bikes, golf clubs, and skis, and the single-car garage is very helpful in harsh winter weather.

Building Style	Quebec Vernacular	**First Floor Area**	1,065 sq. ft.
Bedrooms	3	**Second Floor Area**	536 sq. ft.
Bathrooms	3½	**Total Floor Area**	1,601 sq. ft.
		Bonus Area (Raised Foundation)	915 sq. ft.

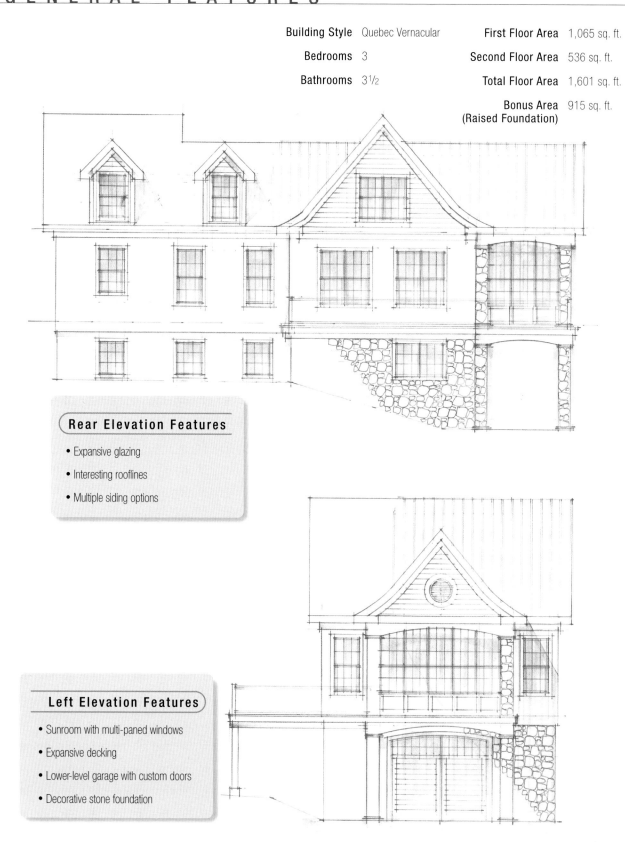

Rear Elevation Features

- Expansive glazing
- Interesting rooflines
- Multiple siding options

Left Elevation Features

- Sunroom with multi-paned windows
- Expansive decking
- Lower-level garage with custom doors
- Decorative stone foundation

The stone walls of the above cottage, like the bell curves of the Franchina Refuge, remind one of early French châteaux. North American cottages have been influenced by the architecture of many areas of Europe. The deep overhangs of many ski chalets mimic Austrian design. The stucco and clay finishes of the Mediterranean are common in southern areas, while the stone cottages of Scotland can be found in the north. Cottages are a melting pot of building techniques from around the world.

Most stone is sold by the pallet and can be used for both landscape and building purposes. The most common types of natural stone used in construction are basalt, gneiss, granite, limestone, sandstone, and slate. These stones come in a wide range of colors and vary in qualities such as weight, grain, workability, and strength. Stone can be installed in its natural shape or be milled to various degrees. It can be readily recycled from old sites with some gentle prying and chipping of old mortar.

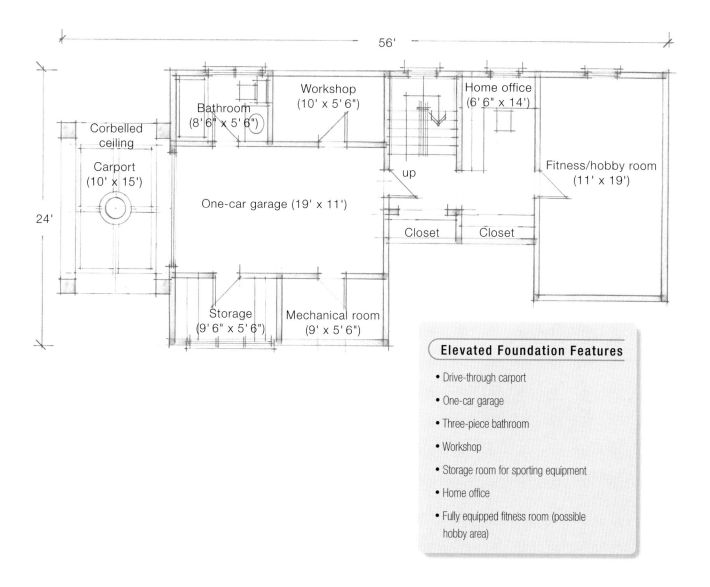

56'

24'

Corbelled
ceiling

Carport
(10' x 15')

Bathroom
(8' 6" x 5' 6")

Workshop
(10' x 5' 6")

Home office
(6' 6" x 14')

up

One-car garage (19' x 11')

Fitness/hobby room
(11' x 19')

Closet

Closet

Storage
(9' 6" x 5' 6")

Mechanical room
(9' x 5' 6")

Elevated Foundation Features

- Drive-through carport
- One-car garage
- Three-piece bathroom
- Workshop
- Storage room for sporting equipment
- Home office
- Fully equipped fitness room (possible hobby area)

Landscaping details

should reflect the materials used in the cottage. This staircase would fit in perfectly with the hilly terrain of the stone-clad Refuge.

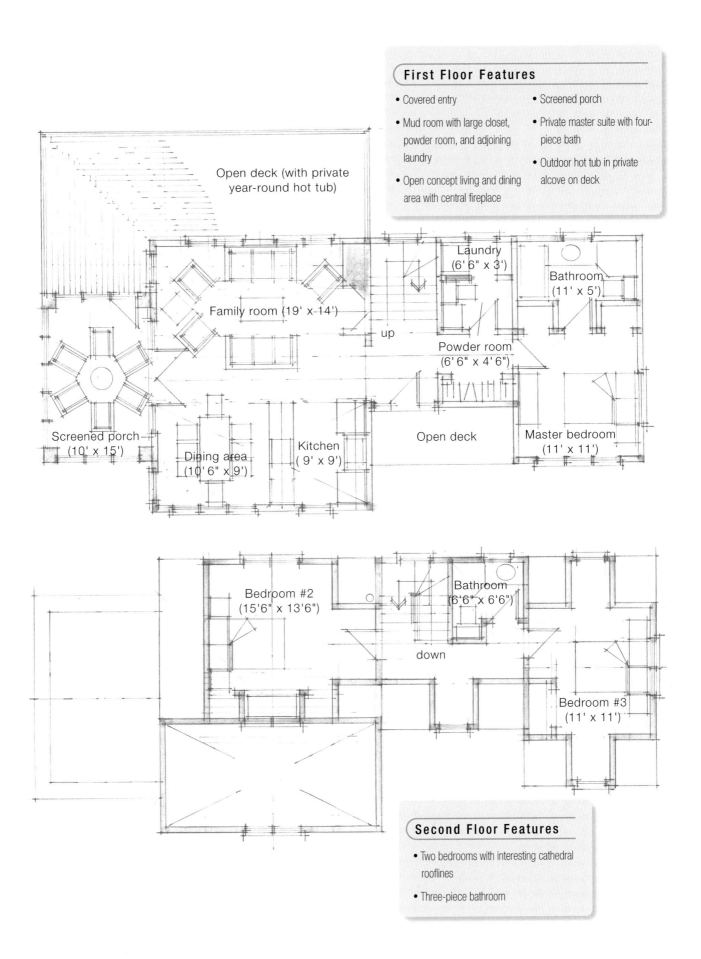

Open deck (with private year-round hot tub)

First Floor Features

- Covered entry

- Mud room with large closet, powder room, and adjoining laundry

- Open concept living and dining area with central fireplace

- Screened porch

- Private master suite with four-piece bath

- Outdoor hot tub in private alcove on deck

Family room (19' x 14')

Laundry
(6' 6" x 3')

Bathroom
(11' x 5')

up

Powder room
(6' 6" x 4' 6")

Screened porch
(10' x 15')

Dining area
(10' 6" x 9')

Kitchen
(9' x 9')

Open deck

Master bedroom
(11' x 11')

Bedroom #2
(15'6" x 13'6")

Bathroom
(6'6" x 6'6")

down

Bedroom #3
(11' x 11')

Second Floor Features

- Two bedrooms with interesting cathedral rooflines

- Three-piece bathroom

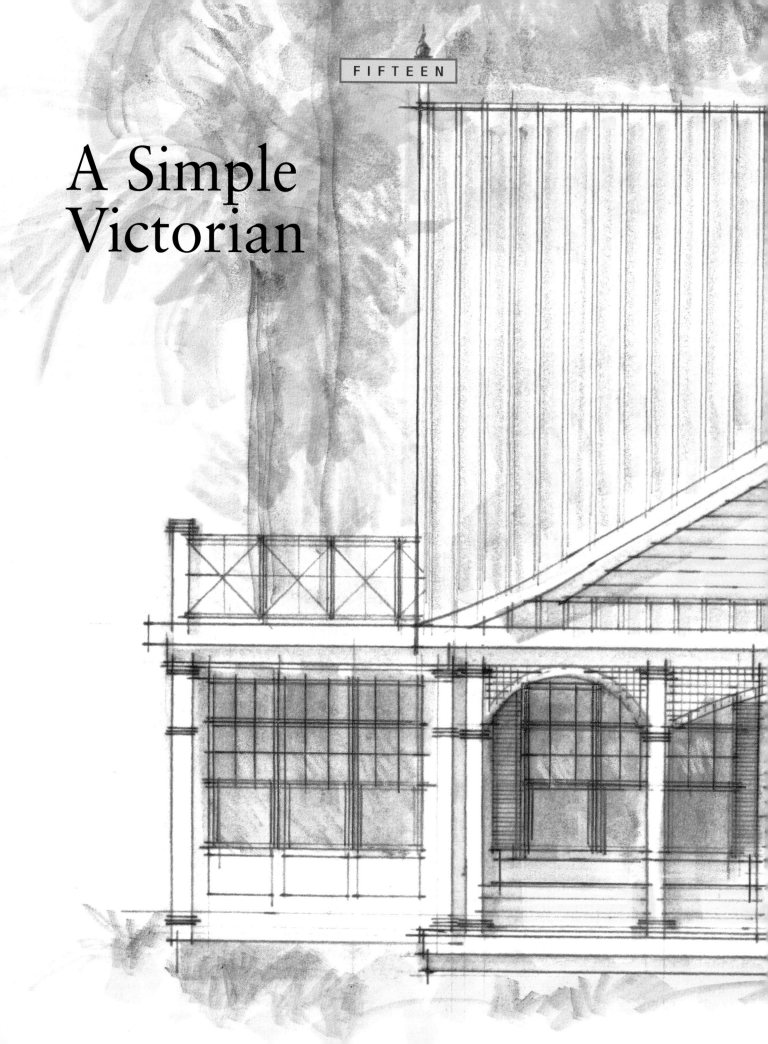

FIFTEEN

A Simple Victorian

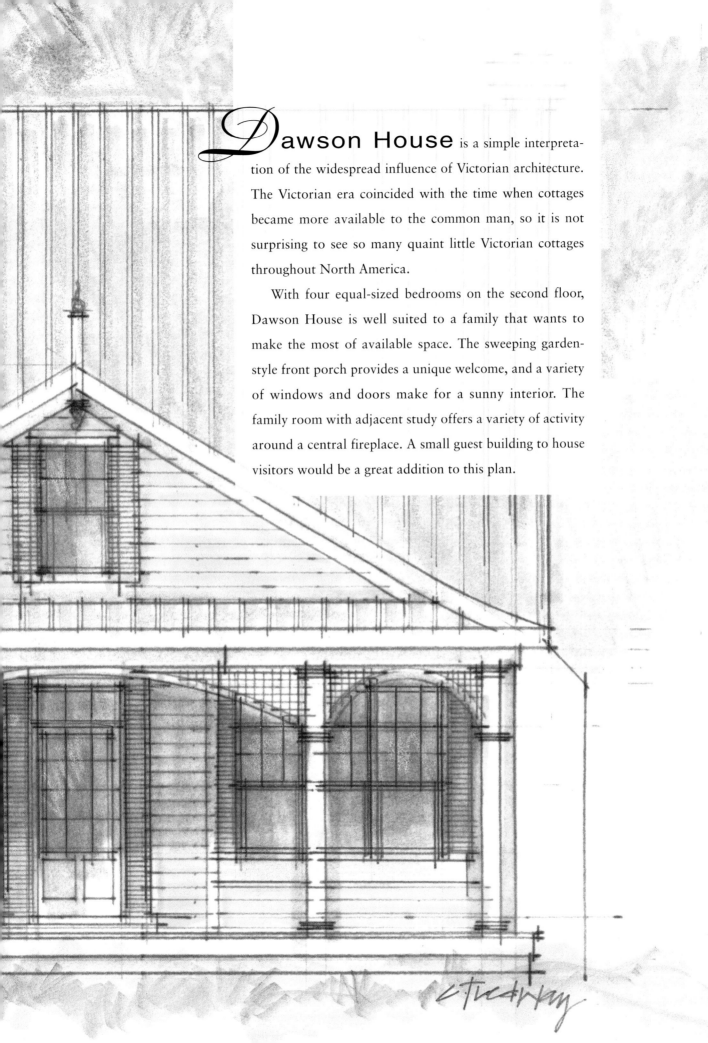

Dawson House is a simple interpretation of the widespread influence of Victorian architecture. The Victorian era coincided with the time when cottages became more available to the common man, so it is not surprising to see so many quaint little Victorian cottages throughout North America.

With four equal-sized bedrooms on the second floor, Dawson House is well suited to a family that wants to make the most of available space. The sweeping garden-style front porch provides a unique welcome, and a variety of windows and doors make for a sunny interior. The family room with adjacent study offers a variety of activity around a central fireplace. A small guest building to house visitors would be a great addition to this plan.

Building Style	Victorian	**First Floor Area**	938 sq. ft.
Bedrooms	4	**Second Floor Area**	792 sq. ft.
Bathrooms	1½	**Total Floor Area**	1,730 sq. ft.

Front Elevation Features

• Sweeping garden-style front porch

• Metal roofing and fine horizontal siding

• Window boxes and shutters

• Nine-foot interior ceilings

• Friendly front entry

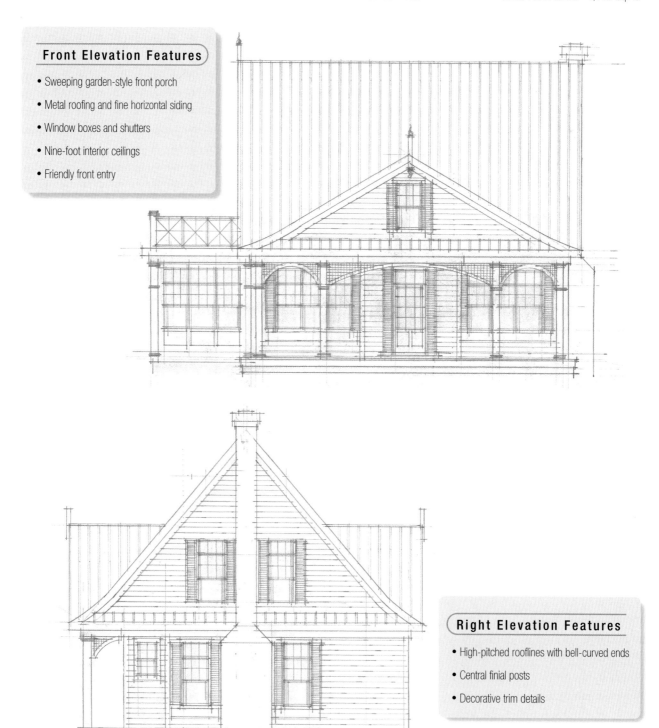

Right Elevation Features

• High-pitched rooflines with bell-curved ends

• Central finial posts

• Decorative trim details

Vents supply fresh air

to attic spaces (left) and are part of the mechanism for proper insulation. In this example, a vent is incorporated into the elegant Victorian detailing. The carved brackets (below left) and finial post (below) are other examples of practical and charming features.

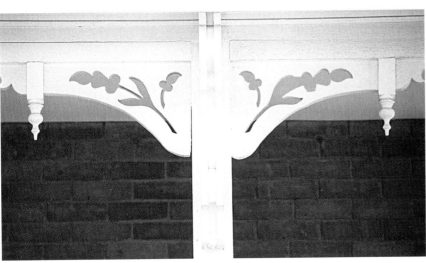

When planning fences

and gates consider the adjacent architecture. This fence would well complement a simple, classic Victorian cottage. It provides enough enclosure for a cozy cottage feeling while remaining relatively open to the street.

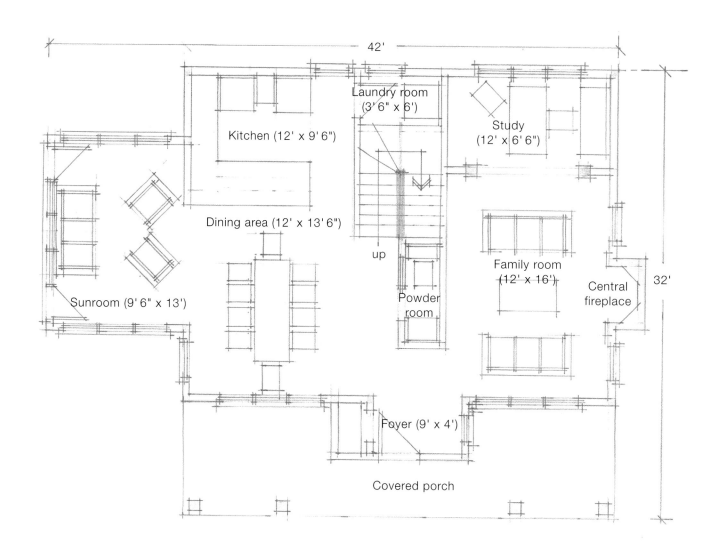

Laundry room
(3' 6" x 6')

Kitchen (12' x 9' 6")

Study
(12' x 6' 6")

Dining area (12' x 13' 6")

up

Family room
(12' x 16')

Central
fireplace

Sunroom (9' 6" x 13')

Powder
room

Foyer (9' x 4')

Covered porch

42'

32'

First Floor Features

- Mud room with bench area and feature window

- Family room with central fireplace

- Study or hobby space open to family room

- Central powder room

- Laundry room off kitchen

- Open concept family room

- Sunroom off dining area

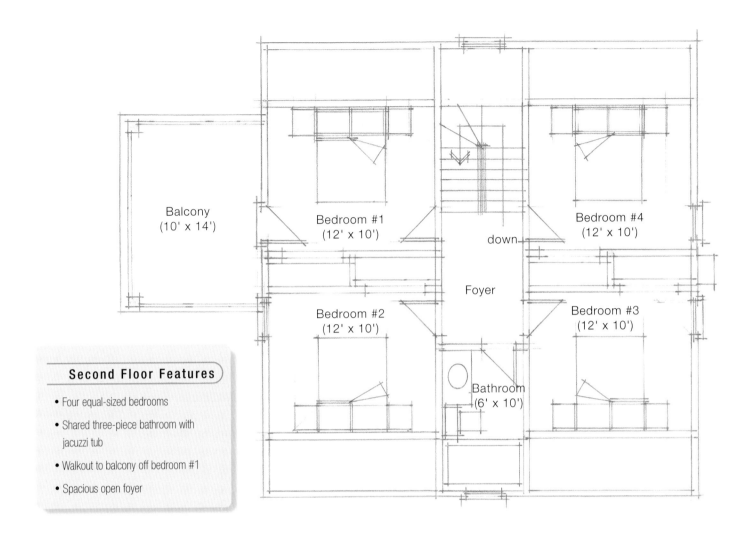

Balcony
(10' x 14')

Bedroom #1
(12' x 10')

down

Bedroom #4
(12' x 10')

Foyer

Bedroom #2
(12' x 10')

Bedroom #3
(12' x 10')

Bathroom
(6' x 10')

Second Floor Features

- Four equal-sized bedrooms

- Shared three-piece bathroom with jacuzzi tub

- Walkout to balcony off bedroom #1

- Spacious open foyer

Railings can be found

in all shapes and styles, from the classic style at right to the rustic, whimsical design at far right. (I love the inset deer cutouts!) Local building codes set limits on heights and allowable openings, but beyond that, the possibilities are endless.

SIXTEEN

A Classic Cottage with Wings

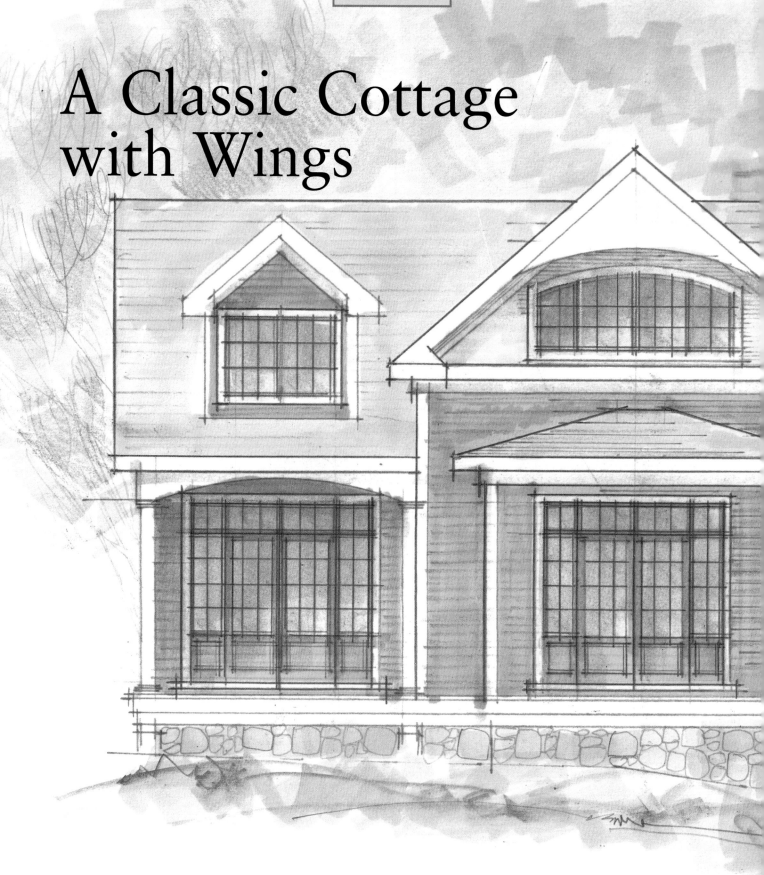

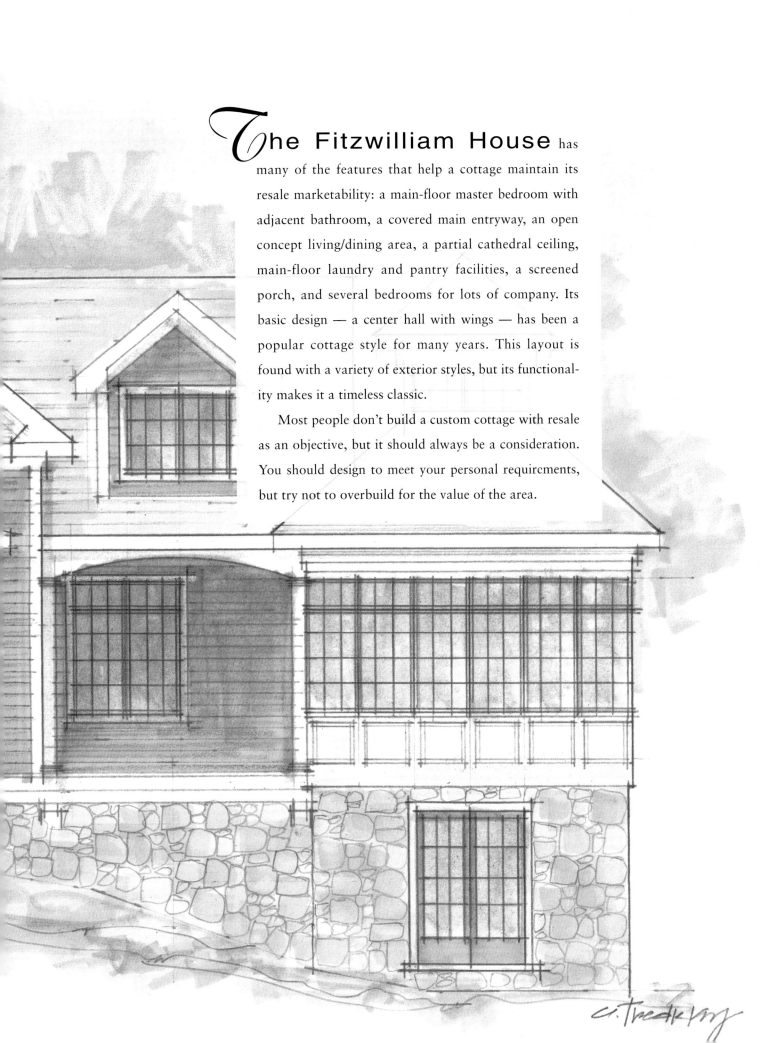

The Fitzwilliam House has

many of the features that help a cottage maintain its resale marketability: a main-floor master bedroom with adjacent bathroom, a covered main entryway, an open concept living/dining area, a partial cathedral ceiling, main-floor laundry and pantry facilities, a screened porch, and several bedrooms for lots of company. Its basic design — a center hall with wings — has been a popular cottage style for many years. This layout is found with a variety of exterior styles, but its functionality makes it a timeless classic.

Most people don't build a custom cottage with resale as an objective, but it should always be a consideration. You should design to meet your personal requirements, but try not to overbuild for the value of the area.

GENERAL FEATURES

Building Style	Shingle Style	**First Floor Area**	1,439 sq. ft.
Bedrooms	4	**Second Floor Area**	775 sq. ft.
Bathrooms	2	**Total Floor Area**	2,214 sq. ft.

Front Elevation Features

- Two covered porches
- Extensive decking
- Feature window
- Transoms above all windows
- Decorative millwork detail and cupola on screened porch
- Optional basement below screened porch

Left Elevation Features

- Shingled end gable
- Interesting dormered roofline
- Awning window above master bed

▲ A basement walkout offers storage for small recreational boats and a lock-up for cottage valuables.

▲ Truly useful basement space requires as many windows as possible.

▲ Stone foundations are attractive but expensive to construct.

The foundation is the critical link that transfers the building load to the ground. Foundations in cottage country may be resting on a variety of soil conditions, rocks, or extreme slopes. Cottage foundations are generally found in three categories: piers, unexcavated, and full. The site, proposed use, and budget will help to determine which foundation is right for you.

As a general rule, people are not basement dwellers, especially when they have decided to spend time in a scenic environment. Sloping lots do offer the availability of full headroom underneath sections of the cottage.

Piers should be used only where soil conditions are stable, wind is not a high factor, the building weight is not excessive, and winter insulation is not a priority. They are cost-effective and can provide a lifetime of stability when properly installed.

Unexcavated foundations offer the ability to skirt the building with an insulated lower wall without taking on a full basement. I recommend this option as a minimum requirement for all sites that will be used year-round in extremely cold or hot climates. The crawl space should always be properly ventilated.

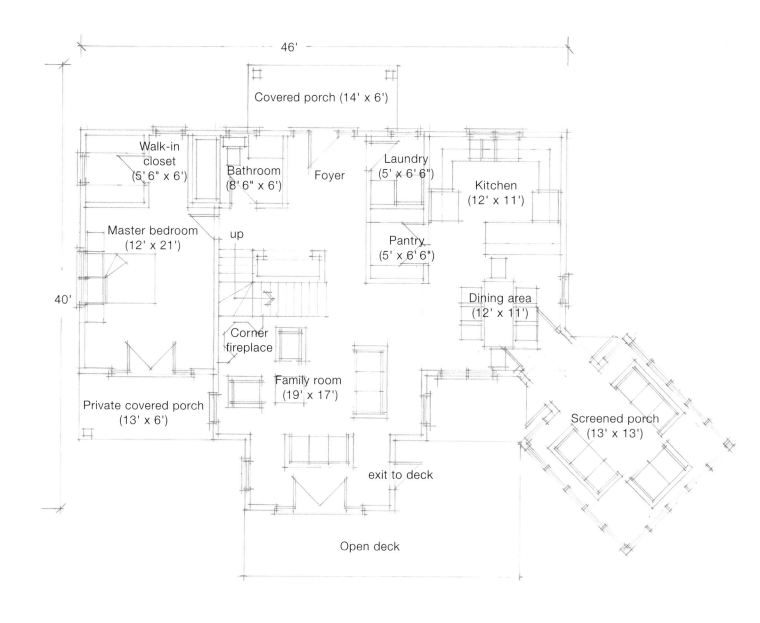

46'

Covered porch (14' x 6')

Walk-in
closet
(5' 6" x 6')

Bathroom
(8' 6" x 6')

Foyer

Laundry
(5' x 6' 6")

Kitchen
(12' x 11')

Master bedroom
(12' x 21')

up

Pantry
(5' x 6' 6")

40'

Dining area
(12' x 11')

Corner
fireplace

Family room
(19' x 17')

Private covered porch
(13' x 6')

Screened porch
(13' x 13')

exit to deck

Open deck

First Floor Features

- Master bedroom with walk-in closet and private covered porch

- Three-piece bathroom

- Laundry and pantry

- Family room with corner fireplace and cathedral ceiling above

- Open concept family/dining areas

- Screened porch with 360-degree views

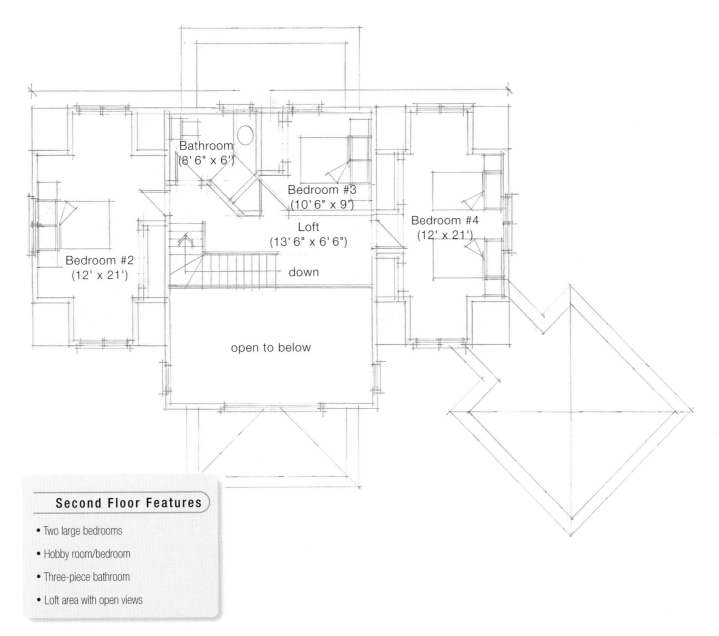

Bathroom
(8' 6" x 6')

Bedroom #3
(10' 6" x 9')

Loft
(13' 6" x 6' 6")

down

Bedroom #4
(12' x 21')

Bedroom #2
(12' x 21')

open to below

Second Floor Features

- Two large bedrooms
- Hobby room/bedroom
- Three-piece bathroom
- Loft area with open views

This gently arching window is known as a camber top. It is an offset detail that well complements the roofline styling of the Fitzwilliam House.

SEVENTEEN

Starter Cottage to Grow With

Claremont Cottage is for anyone who wants to own a first recreational retreat but may not have the budget to complete a large project all at once. If you have been in the market to buy a cottage, your real estate agent has undoubtedly shown you a "starter cottage." Sometimes these are fixer-uppers; sometimes they are just tiny.

A brand-new cottage — not just an older one in severe need of expensive care — can make a perfect, low-cost first cottage. I recommend building small and leaving space for a later addition or else building a two-story building and finishing the main floor only. Claremont Cottage provides all essential living areas on the main floor: a family room, kitchen, bathroom, and bedroom. The structure can be framed and insulated to allow the second-floor space to be finished in the future.

GENERAL FEATURES

Building Style Arts and Crafts

Bedrooms 3 (1 finished, 2 unfinished)

Bathrooms 1½

First Floor Area 1,076 sq. ft.

Second Floor Area 576 sq. ft.

Total Floor Area 1,652 sq. ft.

Front Elevation Features

- Porch across full facade
- Decorative timbers
- Dormers for excellent views from second story

Left Elevation Features

- Central fireplace
- Decorative siding combinations
- Shed porches front and rear with classic railing detail
- Nine-foot main floor height allows for transoms above windows

I have defined the style of Claremont Cottage as Arts and Crafts, but to me it really is just a quintessential cottage. Porches, dormers, sloping second floor spaces, and fireplaces all define the cottage experience. The photos below show some classic cottage details and features.

▲ Entries can be emphasized with sidelights and transoms.

▼ Generous trim and shutters provide instant cottage ambience.

▲ Millwork details from the house should be picked up in adjacent features such as gates and fences.

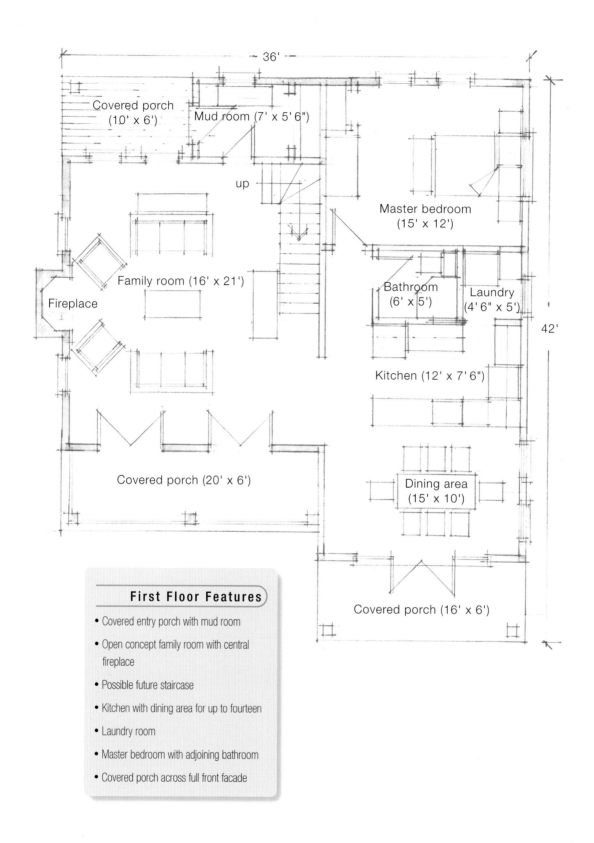

36'

42'

Covered porch
(10' x 6')

Mud room (7' x 5' 6")

up

Master bedroom
(15' x 12')

Family room (16' x 21')

Fireplace

Bathroom
(6' x 5')

Laundry
(4' 6" x 5')

Kitchen (12' x 7' 6")

Covered porch (20' x 6')

Dining area
(15' x 10')

Covered porch (16' x 6')

First Floor Features

- Covered entry porch with mud room
- Open concept family room with central fireplace
- Possible future staircase
- Kitchen with dining area for up to fourteen
- Laundry room
- Master bedroom with adjoining bathroom
- Covered porch across full front facade

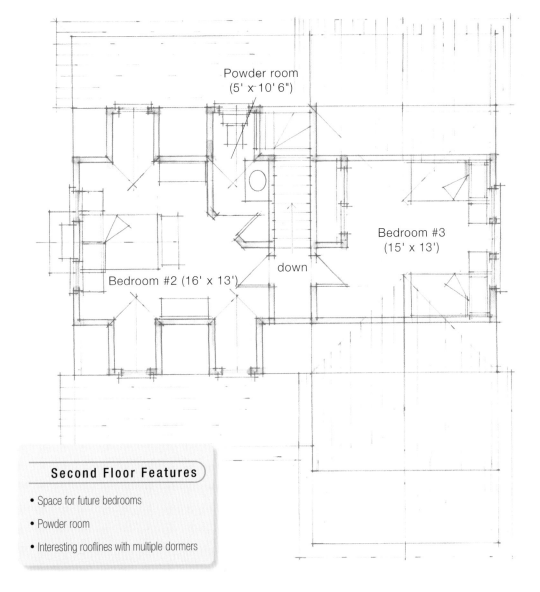

Powder room
(5' x 10' 6")

Bedroom #3
(15' x 13')

down

Bedroom #2 (16' x 13')

Second Floor Features

- Space for future bedrooms

- Powder room

- Interesting rooflines with multiple dormers

Rooflines in cottages

often evolve with quaint and unexpected outcomes. The cottage at left is made of a basic rectangle with a side porch and a front bay bump-out. Claremont Cottage pushes the basic rectangle even further with porches front and rear, bump-out alcoves, dormers, and featured chimneys.

EIGHTEEN

Pet-Friendly Home Away from Home

The Haven House is a Colonial

saltbox, a style originated by early European settlers in the American northeast. The gable-ended roof is one and a half to two stories on one side and one story on the other. This allows for a larger main floor and smaller second-level sleeping quarters. A true saltbox has no roof overhangs or dormers and is usually clad in clapboard or shingles.

This design has been customized to suit the pet-friendly family. Pets at the cottage can present a few extra challenges we don't see at home: lakeside swimming, which brings in extra sand, smelly coats, and water; the pets of overnight guests, who may not get along with your own; lots of excitement, which can make some pets destructive; and extreme temperatures. Pets may also be left for extended periods at the cottage when owners are boating, skiing, or visiting. The Haven House provides a set of design ideas that could easily be applied to other plans to achieve the same results.

Building Style	Colonial Saltbox
Bedrooms	3
Bathrooms	1½
First Floor Area	840 sq. ft.
Second Floor Area	682.5 sq. ft.
Total Floor Area	1,522.5 sq. ft.

Front Elevation Features

- Diamond grill pattern for English country look
- Glass door feature off main dining area
- Generous glass for full views
- Shingle siding

Right Elevation Features

- Standard saltbox with gentle bell-curve roofline
- Stone fireplace

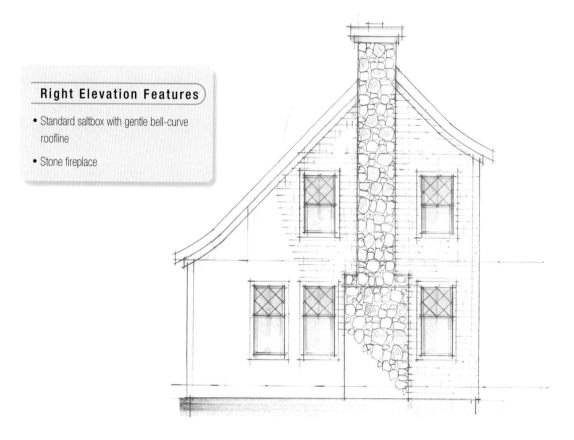

Window trim and shutters provide an opportunity to have fun with both color and detail. Surprisingly, window trim is often overlooked in cottage design. When ordering windows, consider leaving out the stock trim provided; instead, choose an alternative trim to gain a large impact at little additional cost.

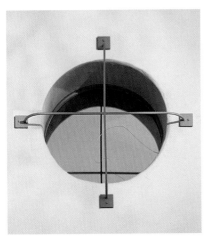

Feature windows are included for light and architectural effect. The smaller windows at left can be functional but are largely for decorative effect.

First Floor Features

- Large front foyer
- Open concept kitchen with dining for up to twelve
- Family room with central fireplace
- Laundry and powder rooms
- Hobby area/workspace

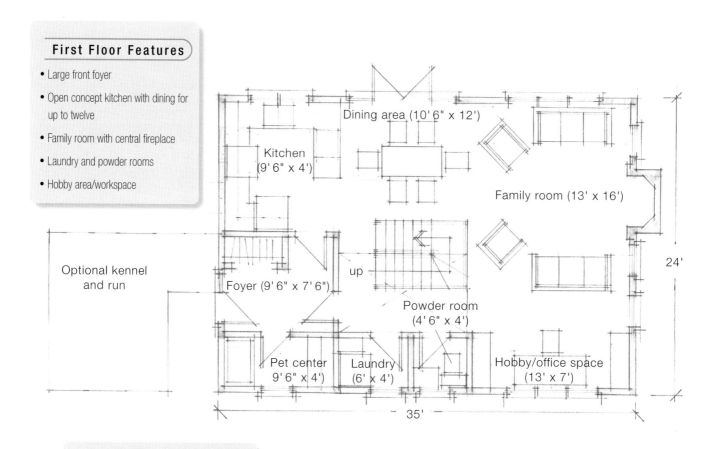

Dining area (10' 6" x 12')

Kitchen (9' 6" x 4')

Family room (13' x 16')

Optional kennel and run

Foyer (9' 6" x 7' 6")

up

Powder room (4' 6" x 4')

Pet center 9' 6" x 4')

Laundry (6' x 4')

Hobby/office space (13' x 7')

24'

35'

Pet Friendly Features

- Outside kennel with attached run and dog door (optionally heated)
- Foyer with pet doors to contain destructive pets, allow for drying time, or separate incompatible pets
- Handheld (hot and cold) shower off the foyer to wash pets
- Pet center for bulk food, feeding, and litter
- Heavy-duty screened door for natural ventilation

A traditional New England cottage, such as the Haven House, could be clad in shingles left to weather naturally.

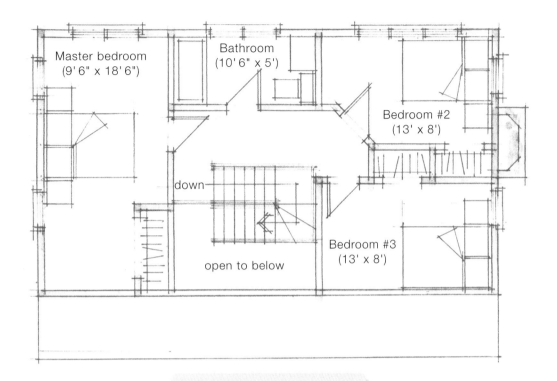

Master bedroom
(9' 6" x 18' 6")

Bathroom
(10' 6" x 5')

Bedroom #2
(13' x 8')

down

open to below

Bedroom #3
(13' x 8')

Second Floor Features

• Three bedrooms with generous storage

• Full bathroom with jet tub

• Spacious hallway open to below

The Saltbox originated

as early as 1670 in the United States. In that period paint was rare, so coloring was limited and came from natural pigment sources. Modern Saltbox cottages often mimic the traditional color combinations of the past. The distinctive long sloping roof was designed to slough off heavy snow and rain. Saltboxes are synonymous with the New England area, but they are surprisingly common across North America.

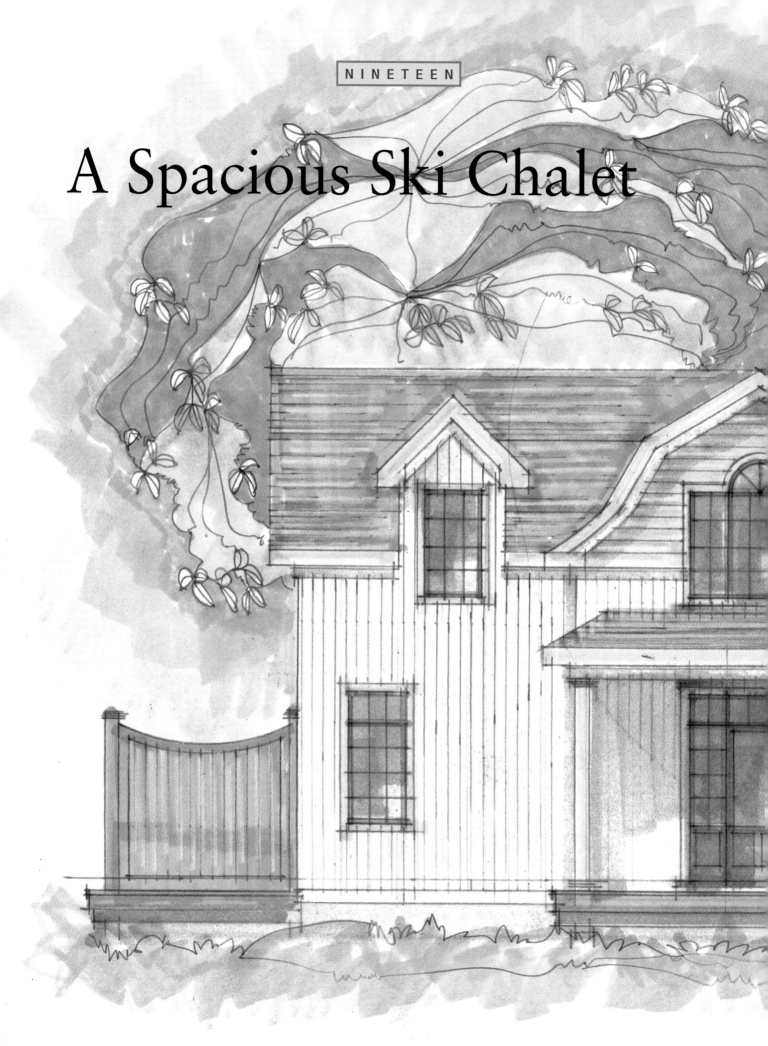

NINETEEN

A Spacious Ski Chalet

𝒯he Acadia House is a classic T-plan with central living and dining areas. The screened porch off the family room extends the gathering areas. I designed the house to be a winter ski retreat with a full spa and outdoor hot tub for après-ski relaxation. The chalet is equipped with four bedrooms for lots of overnight company, and an alcove with adjacent bench provides a perfect ski and boot storage space.

The style of the cottage is referred to as Dutch Colonial or Quebec Vernacular, depending on where it's built. The gambrel roof provides for additional space on the second floor. I have been influenced by this style from its sources in many different areas, but I'm particularly drawn to the brilliant color schemes of the French-Canadian version.

Building Style Dutch Colonial
(Quebec Vernacular)

Bedrooms 4

Bathrooms 2

First Floor Area 968 sq. ft.

Second Floor Area 822 sq. ft.

Total Floor Area 1,790 sq. ft.

Rear Elevation Features

- Generous glazing for full views
- Feature window in upper-level bedroom
- Dormers provide interesting roofline
- Screened porch with views to rear

Right Elevation Features

- Interesting rooflines
- Large upper-level window
- Tall windows with 9-foot interior ceiling

A cottage's doors say a lot to me. The main door in particular should be a focal point: Let it say something about who you are. Traditionally the main door is distinguished by a slightly different color, identifying its relative importance. Special millwork and coverings should also be considered. A home's entry always gives away a little about its occupant's character: tall and impressive, colorful, unusually eccentric, or even staid and traditional.

▲ A wood door with true divided lights with an oval "sunburst" transom in a brick opening.

▲ An insulated four-panel steel door with fluted pilasters and bracketed portico.

▲ Four-panel wood door (referred to as a cross-and-bible design) with transom above.

▲ A solid wood door with classical entablature and traditional colonial color.

▲ Restored wood doors (most likely pine) with original hardware, mail slot, and blasted glass inserts.

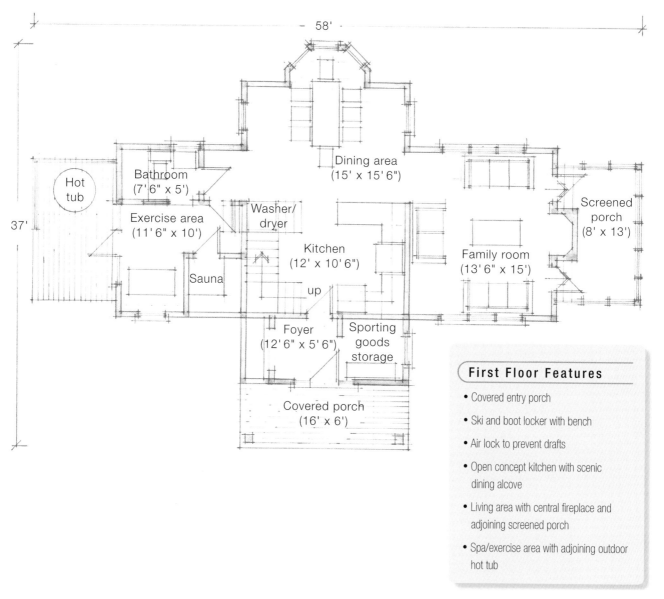

Bathroom
(7' 6" x 5')

Hot tub

Exercise area
(11' 6" x 10')

37'

Washer/
dryer

Dining area
(15' x 15' 6")

Screened
porch
(8' x 13')

Kitchen
(12' x 10' 6")

Sauna

up

Family room
(13' 6" x 15')

Foyer
(12' 6" x 5' 6")

Sporting
goods
storage

Covered porch
(16' x 6')

58'

First Floor Features

• Covered entry porch

• Ski and boot locker with bench

• Air lock to prevent drafts

• Open concept kitchen with scenic dining alcove

• Living area with central fireplace and adjoining screened porch

• Spa/exercise area with adjoining outdoor hot tub

This building is wrapped in a protective vapor barrier and strapped to receive a combination of vertical and horizontal siding similar to that used in the Acadia House. Roof framing is a little delicate when forming the curved end details.

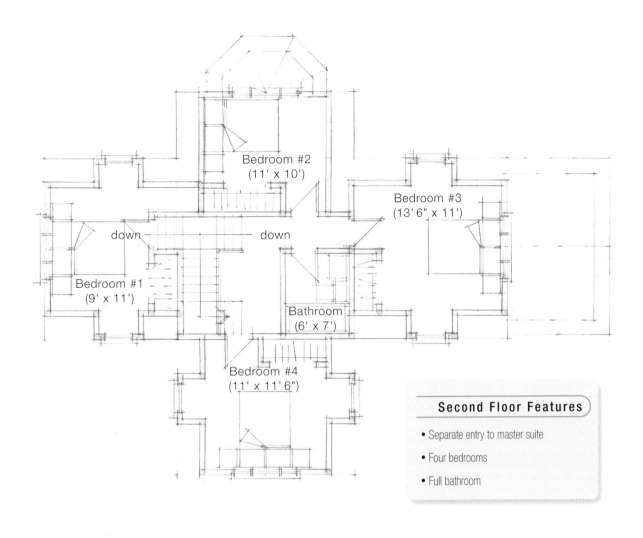

Bedroom #2
(11' x 10')

Bedroom #3
(13' 6" x 11')

down   down

Bedroom #1
(9' x 11')

Bathroom
(6' x 7')

Bedroom #4
(11' x 11' 6")

Second Floor Features

• Separate entry to master suite

• Four bedrooms

• Full bathroom

A change in siding material in the gable end provides a decorative alternative. Such changes usually follow roof or window lines. They can be switches from vertical to horizontal, as on the Acadia House, or a subtle shift to a different horizontal siding, as shown here.

TWENTY

A Musician's Oceanside Retreat

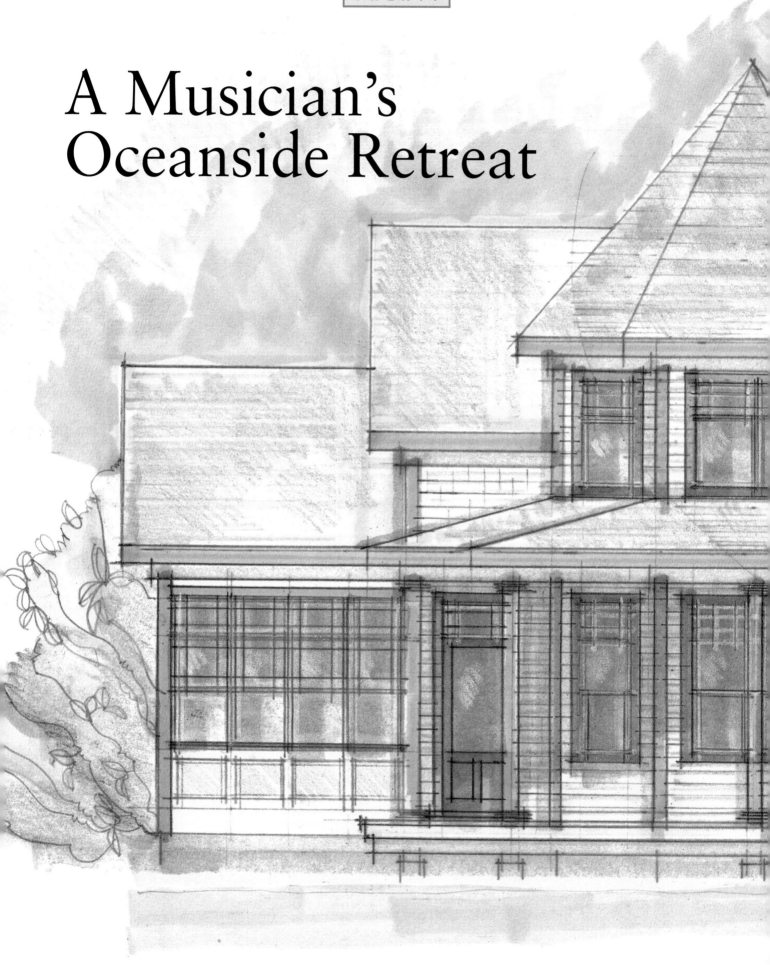

𝒞ornell House takes its influence from the Victorian period. The central turret and wraparound porch are perfect for the delicate detailing associated with this style. Choices of fine details and colors are wide open with Victorian cottages, which often stand out boldly rather than blend into a natural setting. Developments in Florida have especially been influenced by this style. Houses in ice-cream shades with crisp white trim abound. Regional interpretations of this style have spread like wildfire across North America.

This musician's retreat features a small "orchestra balcony" where sound resonates over the cathedral ceiling. A soundproofed recording studio could be substituted for one of the bedrooms or the screened porch. A fireplace and built-in stereo make for relaxing listening under the living room's cathedral dome.

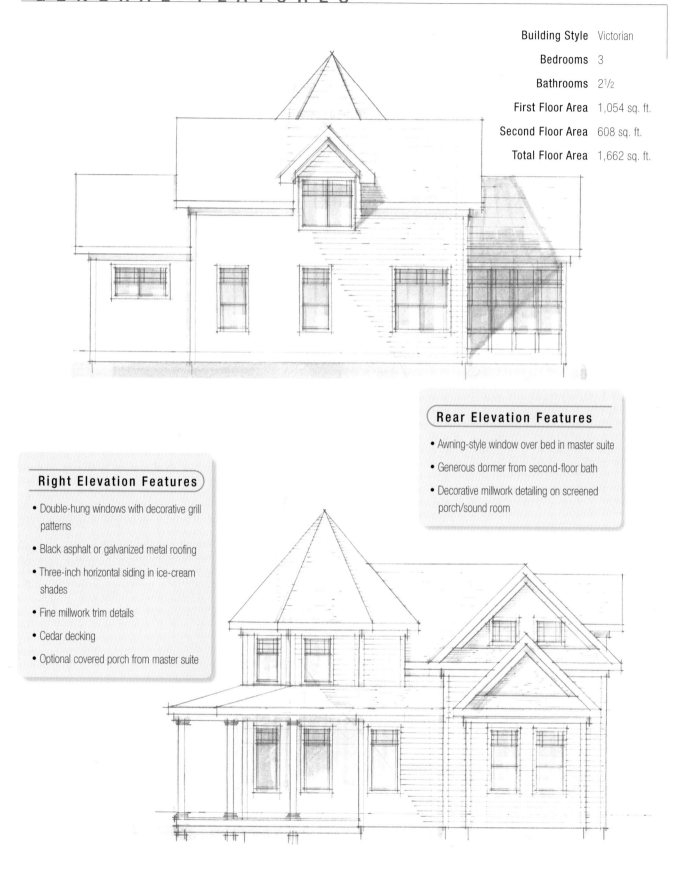

Building Style	Victorian
Bedrooms	3
Bathrooms	2¹/₂
First Floor Area	1,054 sq. ft.
Second Floor Area	608 sq. ft.
Total Floor Area	1,662 sq. ft.

Rear Elevation Features

• Awning-style window over bed in master suite

• Generous dormer from second-floor bath

• Decorative millwork detailing on screened porch/sound room

Right Elevation Features

• Double-hung windows with decorative grill patterns

• Black asphalt or galvanized metal roofing

• Three-inch horizontal siding in ice-cream shades

• Fine millwork trim details

• Cedar decking

• Optional covered porch from master suite

A dramatic turret is an eye-catching feature for any cottage. In locations where you are seeking to maximize the available views, a curved or several-sided room can provide additional windows and unexpected sight lines. It also allows for unusual interior room layouts.

Completely curved turrets such as those pictured at right and below right make the biggest impression, but they are more expensive to construct. Both exterior and interior finishes are more difficult to apply on a curved surface. The turret of the Cornell House, with its four sides, is conventionally built like the porch under construction pictured below. It still makes for an impressive feature at little additional cost.

▲ A lightly finished, shingle-sided turret with decorative millwork in Santa Monica, California.

▲ A wraparound porch under construction with conventional framing methods.

▶ A richly colored turret, shingle-sided with simple millwork in Mt. Tremblant, Quebec.

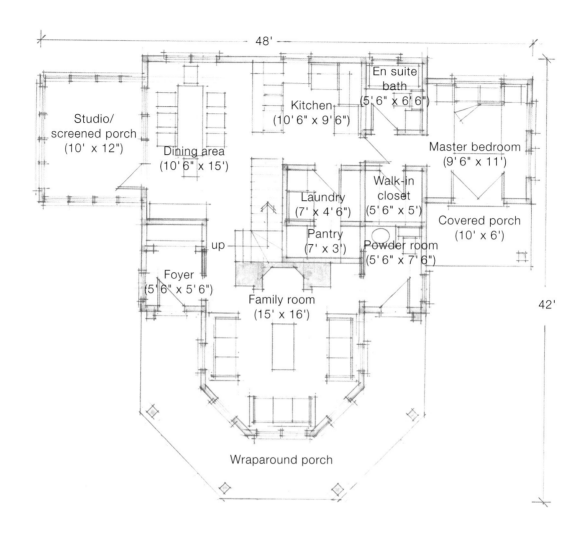

Studio/ screened porch (10' x 12")

Dining area (10' 6" x 15')

Kitchen (10' 6" x 9' 6")

En suite bath (5' 6" x 6' 6")

Master bedroom (9' 6" x 11')

Laundry (7' x 4' 6")

Walk-in closet (5' 6" x 5')

Pantry (7' x 3')

Powder room (5' 6" x 7' 6")

Covered porch (10' x 6')

up

Foyer (5' 6" x 5' 6")

Family room (15' x 16')

Wraparound porch

48'

42'

First Floor Features

- Turreted living space with full cathedral ceiling

- Wraparound porch

- Direct exterior access to washroom from beach

- Mudroom with closet for storing coats and sporting goods

- Fireplace with built-ins to house music system

- Dining area to seat up to twelve

- Open concept kitchen with adjoining laundry room and pantry

- Screened porch or optional sound studio

- Master suite on main floor with bath/jacuzzi tub, walk-in closet, and French doors to private covered porch

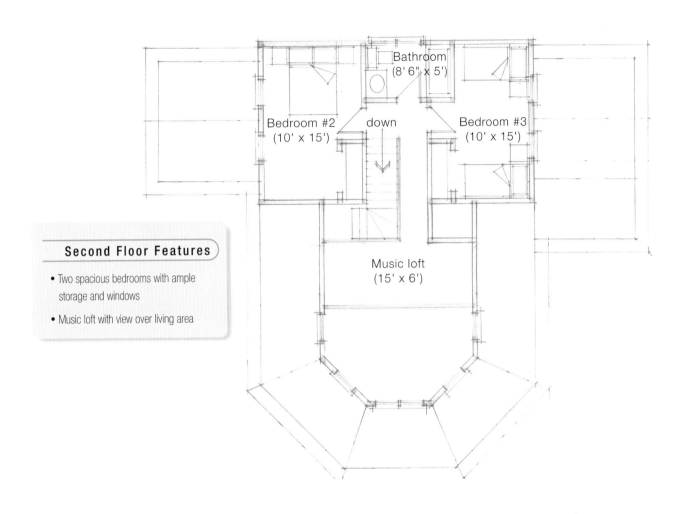

Bathroom
(8' 6" x 5')

Bedroom #2
(10' x 15')

down

Bedroom #3
(10' x 15')

Music loft
(15' x 6')

Second Floor Features

- Two spacious bedrooms with ample storage and windows
- Music loft with view over living area

The local grasses, birds, and sky of a seaside area can inspire a restful selection of colors to give your cottage the proper mood.

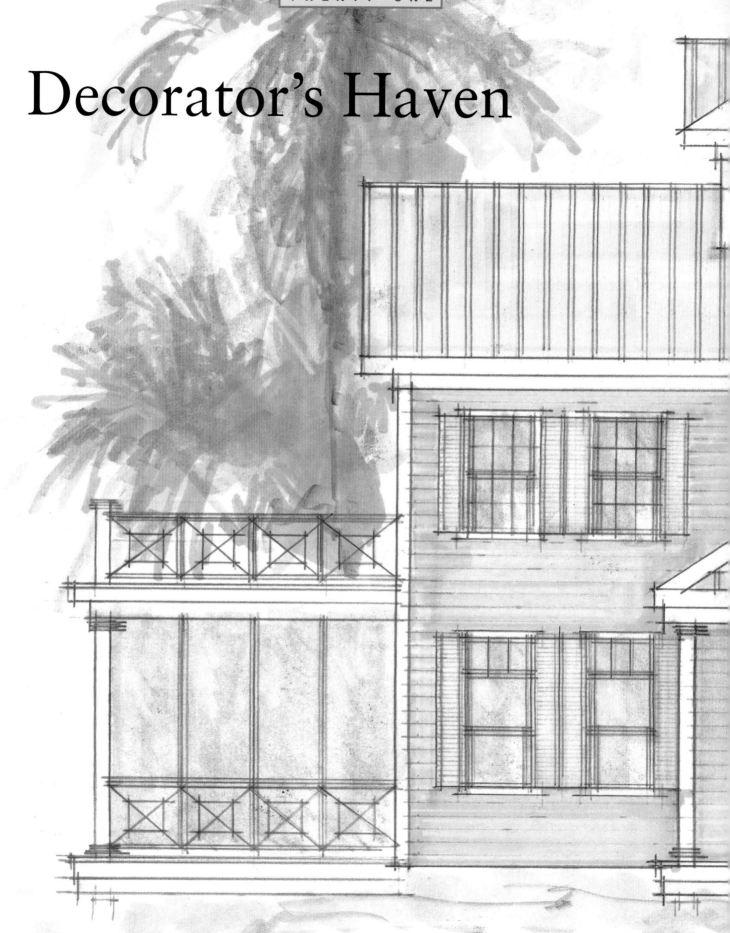

TWENTY-ONE

Decorator's Haven

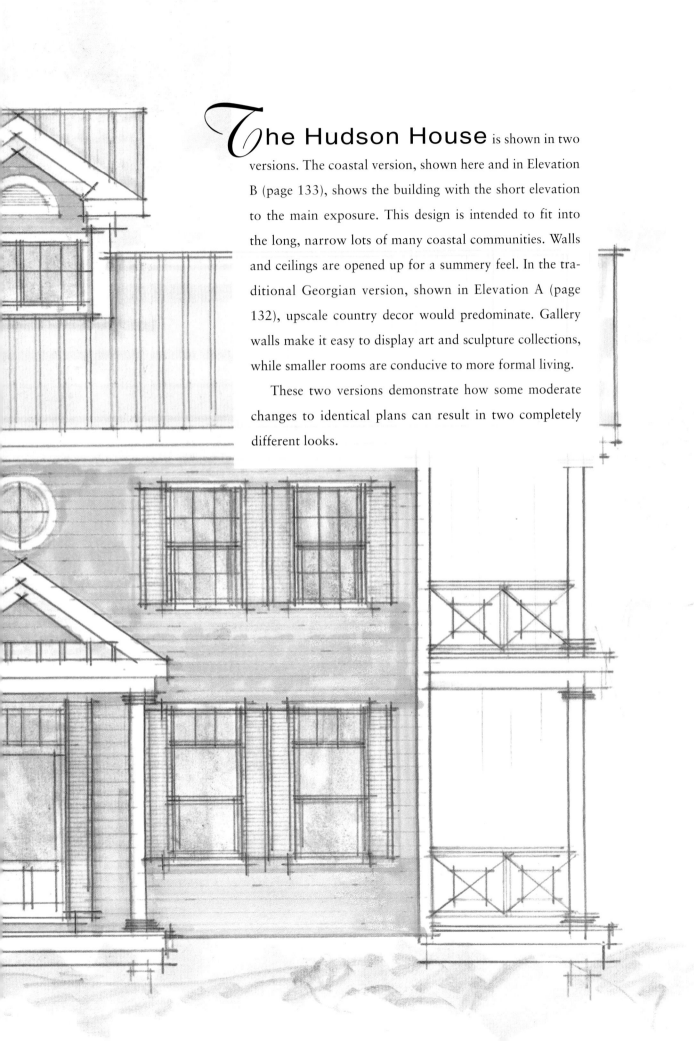

*T*he Hudson House is shown in two versions. The coastal version, shown here and in Elevation B (page 133), shows the building with the short elevation to the main exposure. This design is intended to fit into the long, narrow lots of many coastal communities. Walls and ceilings are opened up for a summery feel. In the traditional Georgian version, shown in Elevation A (page 132), upscale country decor would predominate. Gallery walls make it easy to display art and sculpture collections, while smaller rooms are conducive to more formal living.

These two versions demonstrate how some moderate changes to identical plans can result in two completely different looks.

GENERAL FEATURES

Building Style Georgian or
Southern Coastal

Bedrooms 3

Bathrooms 2

First Floor Area 886 sq. ft.

Second Floor Area 650 sq. ft.

Total Floor Area 1,536 sq. ft.

Front Elevation Features "A"

- Classic Georgian proportion
- Majestic front porch
- Geared to wide front exposure
- Classic white siding recommended
- High-quality black asphalt roof with clean lines

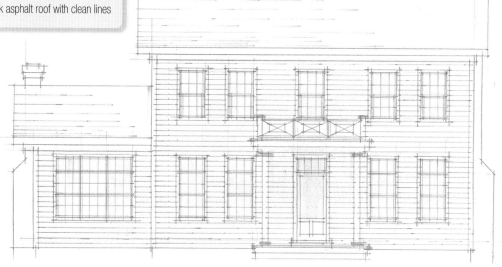

Left Elevation Features "A"

- Sunroom with high-quality millwork panel detail
- Walk-out to garden terrace, pergola above

Front Elevation Features "B"

• Geared to narrow front exposure

• Balconies from first and second level

• Pastel-colored finish recommended

• Metal roofing with multilevel detail

• Cupola above

Classic Georgian proportion and balanced window configuration lend elegance to this home. As would be appropriate with the Georgian-style Elevation "A" design on the opposite page, the broad front of the house faces into a nicely landscaped yard enclosed by a picket fence.

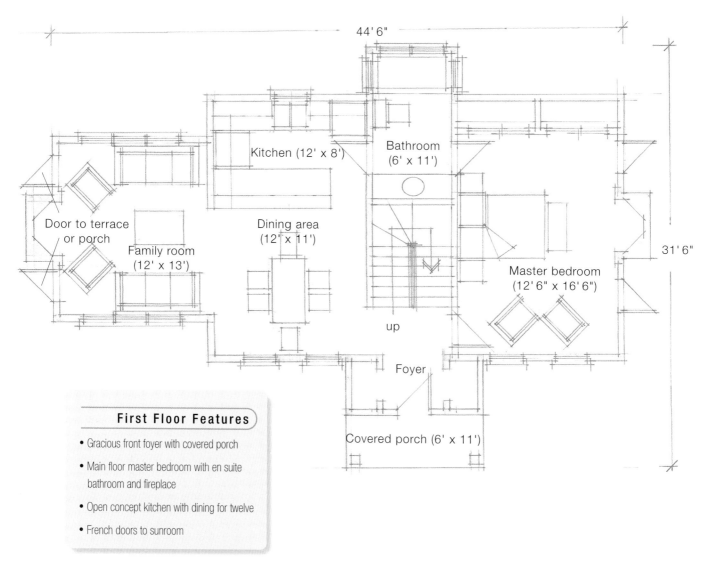

44' 6"

Kitchen (12' x 8')

Bathroom
(6' x 11')

Door to terrace
or porch

Dining area
(12' x 11')

Family room
(12' x 13')

Master bedroom
(12' 6" x 16' 6")

31' 6"

up

Foyer

Covered porch (6' x 11')

First Floor Features

- Gracious front foyer with covered porch
- Main floor master bedroom with en suite bathroom and fireplace
- Open concept kitchen with dining for twelve
- French doors to sunroom

Stairs provide flow

between floors and are important to the building's overall space plan. Cottage layouts tend to be unusual, as they try to fit themselves to unique site and view requirements. Stairs take up a significant amount of space and should be integrated from the beginning to meet both the practical and the aesthetic needs of the cottage. Building departments across North America dictate safety and structural requirements surrounding stair construc-

tion, so be certain to consult with local authorities before determining the details of this central piece of your interior layout.

Practical considerations aside, the staircase can be a fun and central feature of any building. Open or closed risers, stair materials, views, railing details, and finishing details all provide an endless spectrum of choices. Visit as many cottages and showrooms as possible and use design magazines to inspire you to think outside the ordinary.

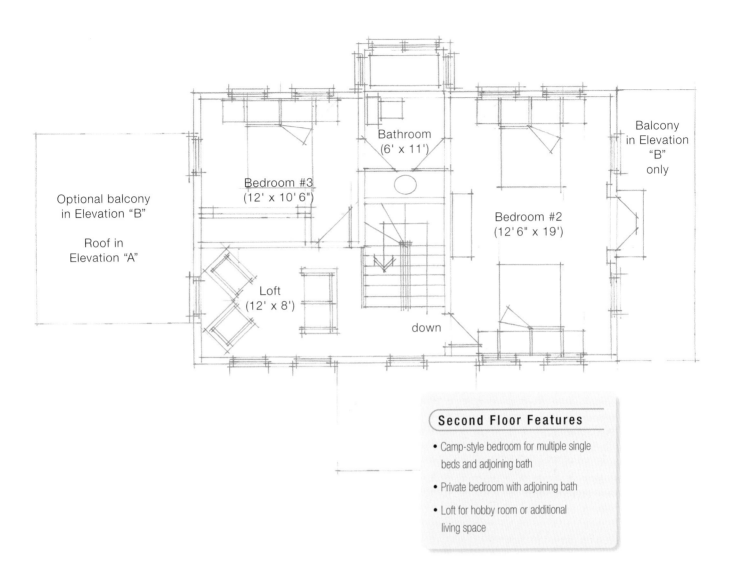

Bathroom
(6' x 11')

Balcony
in Elevation
"B"
only

Optional balcony
in Elevation "B"

Roof in
Elevation "A"

Bedroom #3
(12' x 10' 6")

Bedroom #2
(12' 6" x 19')

Loft
(12' x 8')

down

Second Floor Features

• Camp-style bedroom for multiple single
beds and adjoining bath

• Private bedroom with adjoining bath

• Loft for hobby room or additional
living space

▲ Tile stairs can be used indoors or out. Use a variety of colors to create
interesting patterns.

▲ Brick can be used as an interior finish but is more common outside.
Choose a good-quality solid brick. Reclaimed brick tends to crumble
when used in extreme climates. Brick slices are great for interior flooring,
as they have rustic appeal without excessive weight.

TWENTY-TWO

Island Honeymoon Hideaway

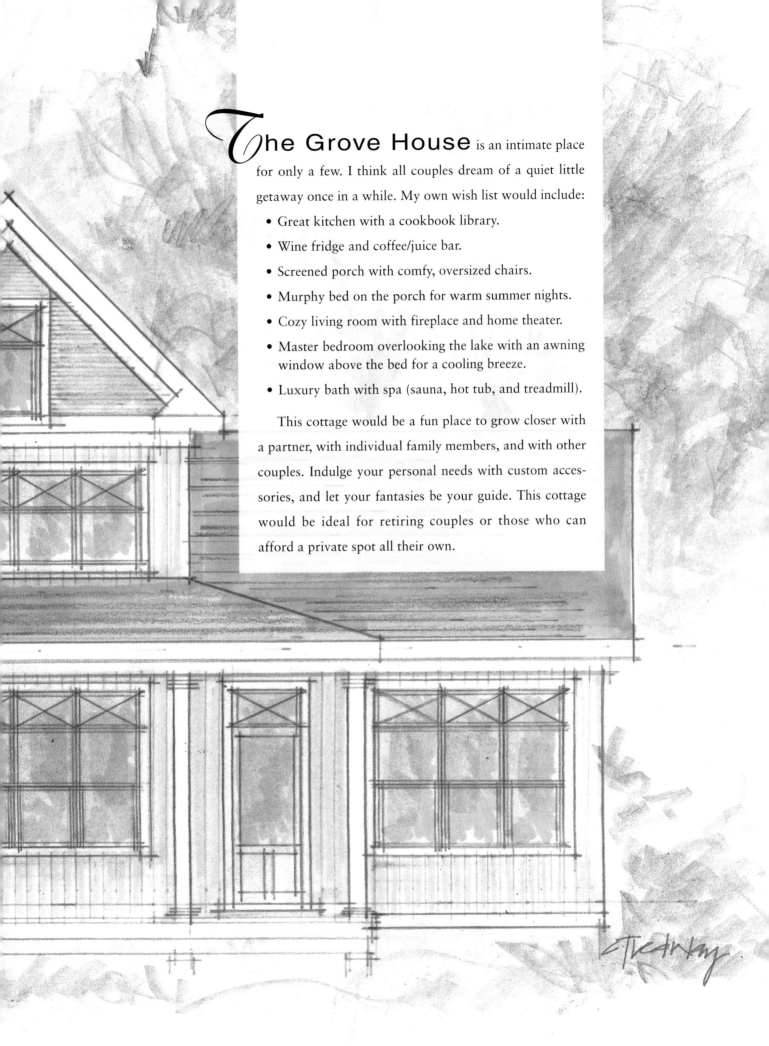

𝒯he Grove House is an intimate place for only a few. I think all couples dream of a quiet little getaway once in a while. My own wish list would include:

- Great kitchen with a cookbook library.
- Wine fridge and coffee/juice bar.
- Screened porch with comfy, oversized chairs.
- Murphy bed on the porch for warm summer nights.
- Cozy living room with fireplace and home theater.
- Master bedroom overlooking the lake with an awning window above the bed for a cooling breeze.
- Luxury bath with spa (sauna, hot tub, and treadmill).

This cottage would be a fun place to grow closer with a partner, with individual family members, and with other couples. Indulge your personal needs with custom accessories, and let your fantasies be your guide. This cottage would be ideal for retiring couples or those who can afford a private spot all their own.

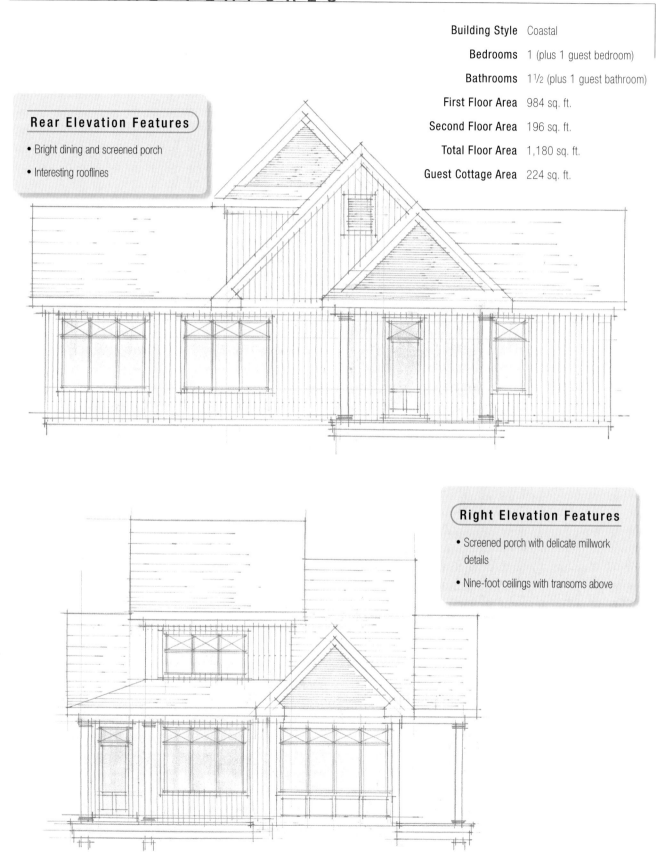

Building Style   Coastal

Bedrooms   1 (plus 1 guest bedroom)

Bathrooms   1½ (plus 1 guest bathroom)

First Floor Area   984 sq. ft.

Second Floor Area   196 sq. ft.

Total Floor Area   1,180 sq. ft.

Guest Cottage Area   224 sq. ft.

Rear Elevation Features

• Bright dining and screened porch

• Interesting rooflines

Right Elevation Features

• Screened porch with delicate millwork details

• Nine-foot ceilings with transoms above

Serene lake views such as the one above can be enhanced by a cottage with second-level lookouts (left) in the most dramatic directions. When siting a cottage for views, it is important to consider how views will change seasonally with the growth of leaves in spring and the bare trees of late autumn and winter.

A screened porch is a perfect spot for spending a quiet night with a glass of wine. A creative use of millwork from the porch roof through the doors and windows, and on down to the foundation, gives this porch a classic look.

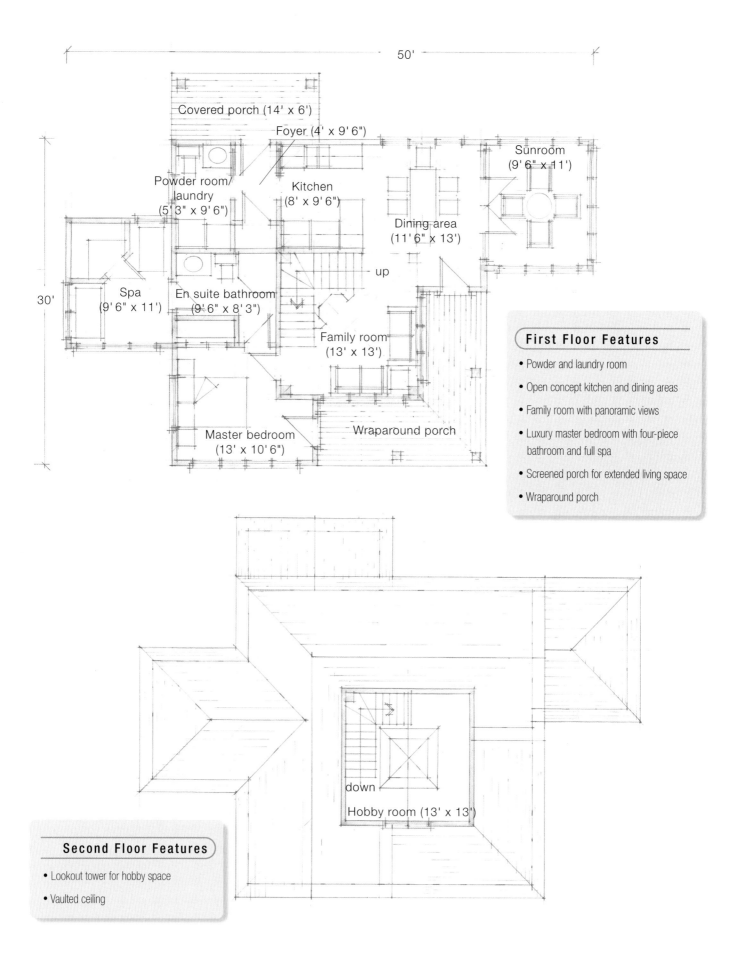

Covered porch (14' x 6')

Foyer (4' x 9' 6")

Sunroom
(9' 6" x 11')

Powder room/
laundry
(5' 3" x 9' 6")

Kitchen
(8' x 9' 6")

Dining area
(11' 6" x 13')

50'

30'

Spa
(9' 6" x 11')

En suite bathroom
(9' 6" x 8' 3")

up

Family room
(13' x 13')

Master bedroom
(13' x 10' 6")

Wraparound porch

First Floor Features

- Powder and laundry room
- Open concept kitchen and dining areas
- Family room with panoramic views
- Luxury master bedroom with four-piece bathroom and full spa
- Screened porch for extended living space
- Wraparound porch

down

Hobby room (13' x 13')

Second Floor Features

- Lookout tower for hobby space
- Vaulted ceiling

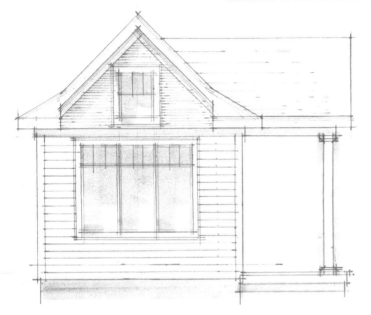

Front Elevation

Right Elevation

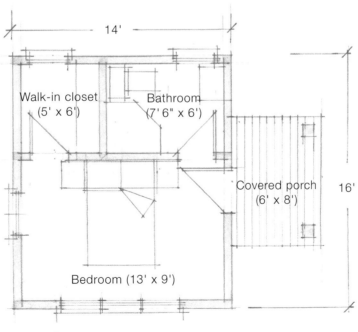

14'

Walk-in closet
(5' x 6')

Bathroom
(7'6" x 6')

Covered porch
(6' x 8')

16'

Bedroom (13' x 9')

Floor Plan

TWENTY-THREE

A Shipbuilder's Pride

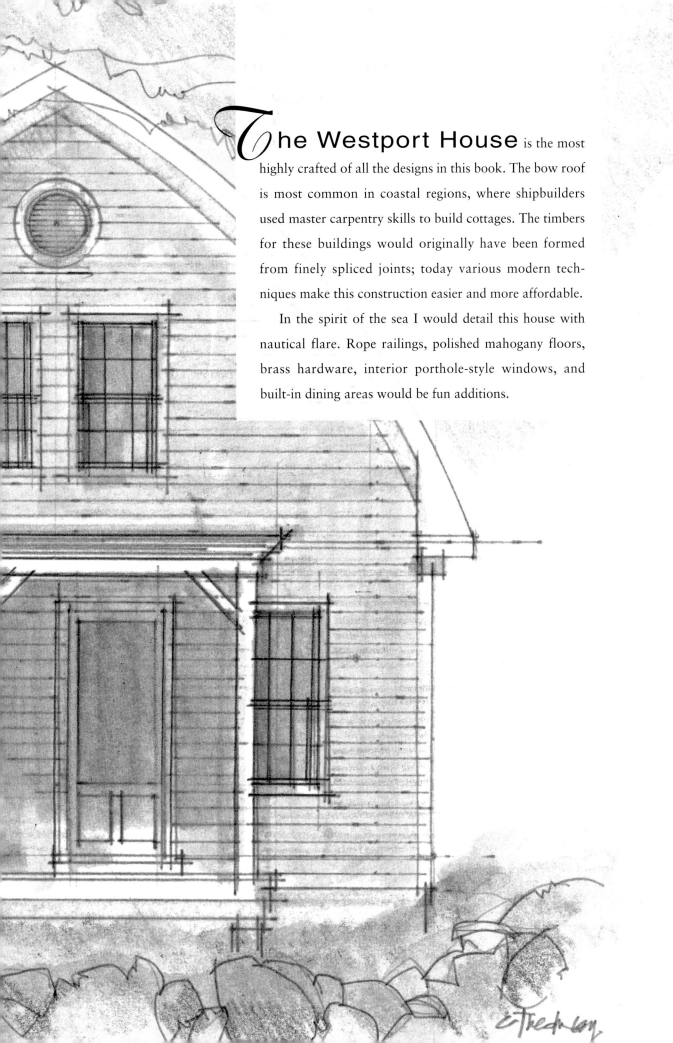

*T*he Westport House is the most highly crafted of all the designs in this book. The bow roof is most common in coastal regions, where shipbuilders used master carpentry skills to build cottages. The timbers for these buildings would originally have been formed from finely spliced joints; today various modern techniques make this construction easier and more affordable.

In the spirit of the sea I would detail this house with nautical flare. Rope railings, polished mahogany floors, brass hardware, interior porthole-style windows, and built-in dining areas would be fun additions.

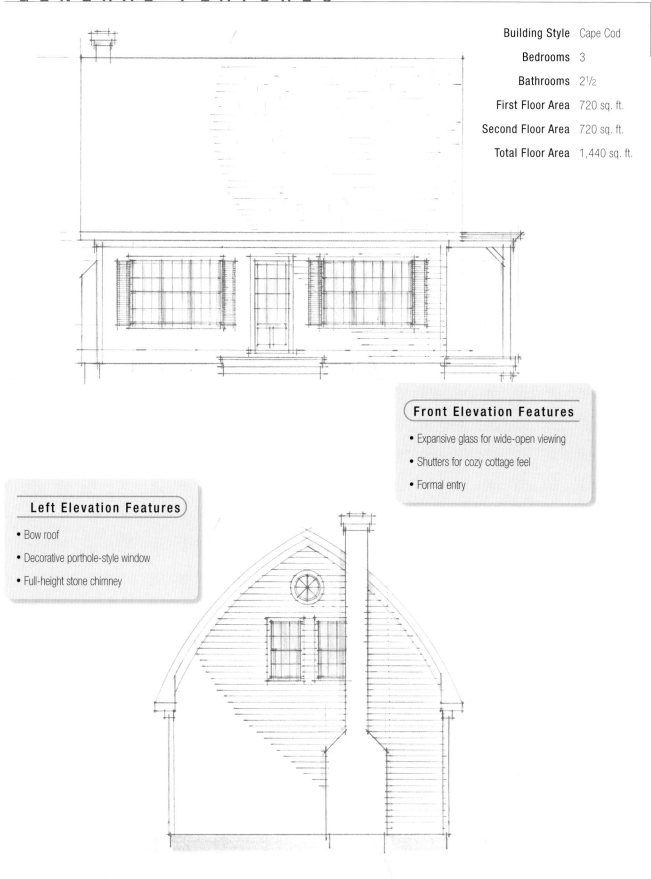

Building Style	Cape Cod
Bedrooms	3
Bathrooms	2½
First Floor Area	720 sq. ft.
Second Floor Area	720 sq. ft.
Total Floor Area	1,440 sq. ft.

Front Elevation Features

- Expansive glass for wide-open viewing
- Shutters for cozy cottage feel
- Formal entry

Left Elevation Features

- Bow roof
- Decorative porthole-style window
- Full-height stone chimney

The smell of a crackling fire always brings me instant peace, and a place to build a fire is unmistakably the most common request in cottage design. A fireplace is the heart of the living room in the Westport House and in many other cottages in this book. Fireplaces come in all shapes and sizes, made of stone, stucco, tile, you name it. Modern technology also allows for such installations as zero clearance, gas, electric, or traditional masonry. Wood fireplaces are known for their smell and penetrating warmth. Gas fireplaces provide easy starts and a heat source as efficient as a furnace. Electric units are surprisingly economical to run, although they provide little warmth. Masonry units offer the widest options of styles, but they tend to be inefficient in heat conservation.

Preconstructed models are generally cheaper than units built at the site. Personally, I recommend buying from a higher-quality manufacturer that casts facings and freestanding units into attractive, time-tested designs.

Exterior fireplaces have recently become more common. Take extra caution to avoid canopy vegetation when locating such a fireplace.

Wood-burning or gas stoves are synonymous with rustic settings and work well in limited spaces. Newer wood stoves offer advanced technology and designs that limit environmental impact and maximize heat output.

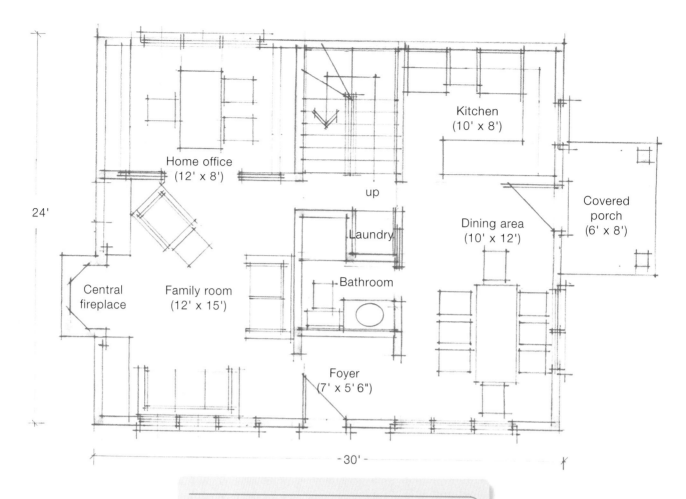

Home office
(12' x 8')

Kitchen
(10' x 8')

up

Covered
porch
(6' x 8')

24'

Laundry

Dining area
(10' x 12')

Central
fireplace

Family room
(12' x 15')

Bathroom

Foyer
(7' x 5' 6")

- 30' -

First Floor Features

- Covered entry porch

- Family room with central fireplace

- Optional porthole-style windows
  between home office and family
  room

- Optional built-in boat-style seating

- Laundry area

- Open concept kitchen/dining area

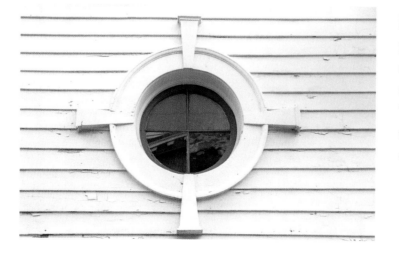

Round windows in a
porthole style make a great
addition to a seaside cottage
such as the Westport House.
These details give a building
the romantic feel of a home
on the ocean.

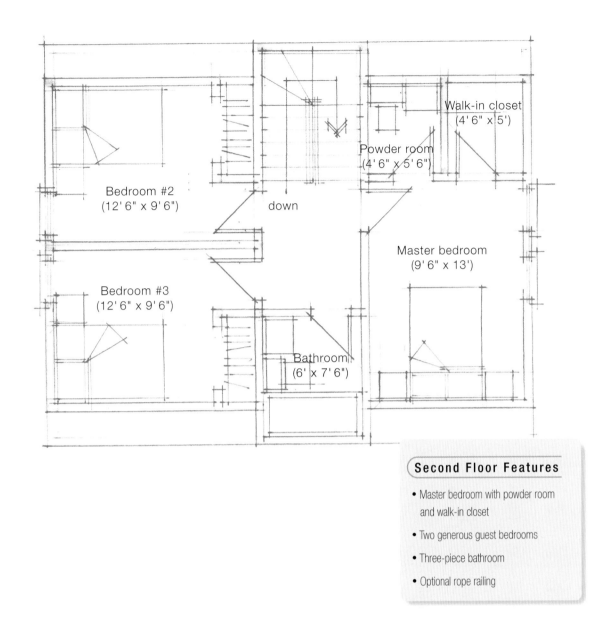

Bedroom #2
(12' 6" x 9' 6")

down

Powder room
(4' 6" x 5' 6")

Walk-in closet
(4' 6" x 5')

Bedroom #3
(12' 6" x 9' 6")

Master bedroom
(9' 6" x 13')

Bathroom
(6' x 7' 6")

Second Floor Features

• Master bedroom with powder room and walk-in closet

• Two generous guest bedrooms

• Three-piece bathroom

• Optional rope railing

Cape Cod style commonly has simple rooflines, horizontal siding, fine millwork, and classic proportioning. For a cottage it is an excellent building block to start with, as it allows for simple additions. Rambling versions of this style are common throughout New England. These cottages often tell a story of the growth of a family.

A bow roof, as shown in the Westport House and at right, is a relatively uncommon feature on a Cape Cod–style cottage. If you are considering building a cottage with this roof, try pricing your design with a timber frame or truss company to see if it can be done for a reasonable cost.

Roof systems are not just aesthetic features; they also control the flow of water, air, heat, and cold above and around a cottage. They must be designed to span across open spaces and hold their own weight plus the stresses caused by wind, snow, and rain. Many cottagers favor roofs with open rafters, which provide greater space but also present special challenges to the structural and insulation systems. Modern technologies offer more opportunities than ever to push structural boundaries and eliminate the need for supporting columns and walls.

As for many parts of the building, local codes will dictate minimal requirements for the roof. Climate is a strong factor in roofing choices, and requirements vary widely across North America. Economics, ease of maintenance, and visual appeal should all be considered when you are choosing one roof style over another.

Some practical items to consider, regardless of where your cottage is located:

- Flat roofs require a continuous membrane material.
- Sloping roofs shed water and snow more easily.
- Watch for converging rooflines, and make certain there is proper drainage.
- Supply added protection, such as flashing, to areas that will have continuous snow or water flow.
- Certain roof shapes are closely associated with different architectural styles, so try to be consistent in your choices. On these pages I've provided a visual glossary of the main styles of roofs found in cottages.

Gable. A roof sloping downward in two parts from a central ridge, forming a flat triangulated area at each end.

Side view

Front view

Hip. A roof sloping off in four directions.

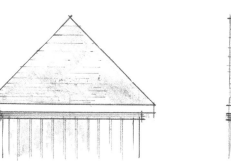

Side view

Front view

Traditional Cottage. A hip/gable combination with gable at top.

Side view

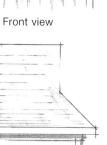

Front view

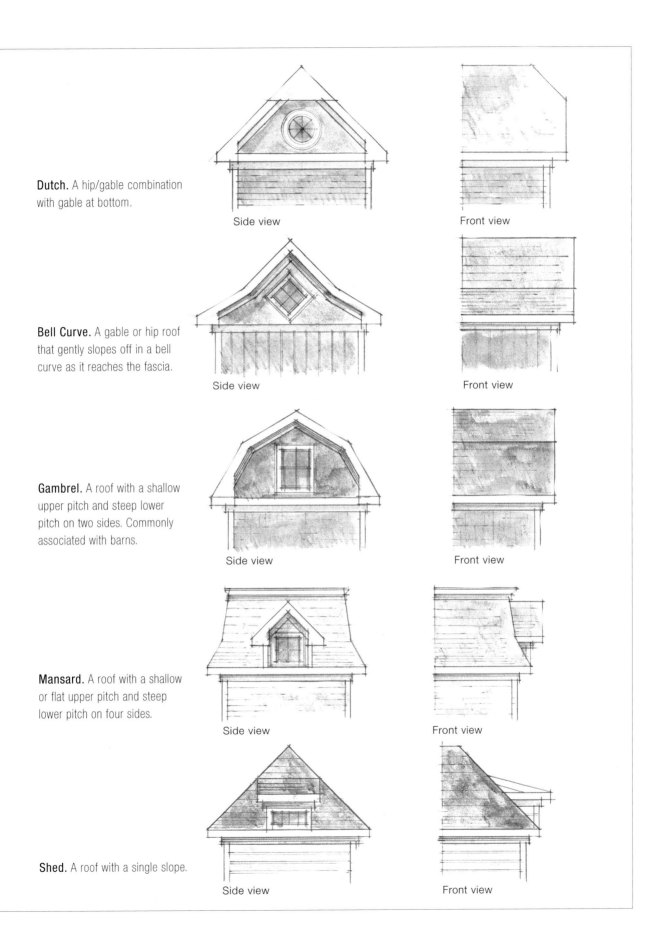

Dutch. A hip/gable combination with gable at bottom.

Side view
Front view

Bell Curve. A gable or hip roof that gently slopes off in a bell curve as it reaches the fascia.

Side view
Front view

Gambrel. A roof with a shallow upper pitch and steep lower pitch on two sides. Commonly associated with barns.

Side view
Front view

Mansard. A roof with a shallow or flat upper pitch and steep lower pitch on four sides.

Side view
Front view

Shed. A roof with a single slope.

Side view
Front view

TWENTY-FOUR

A Retreat Inspired by Hemingway

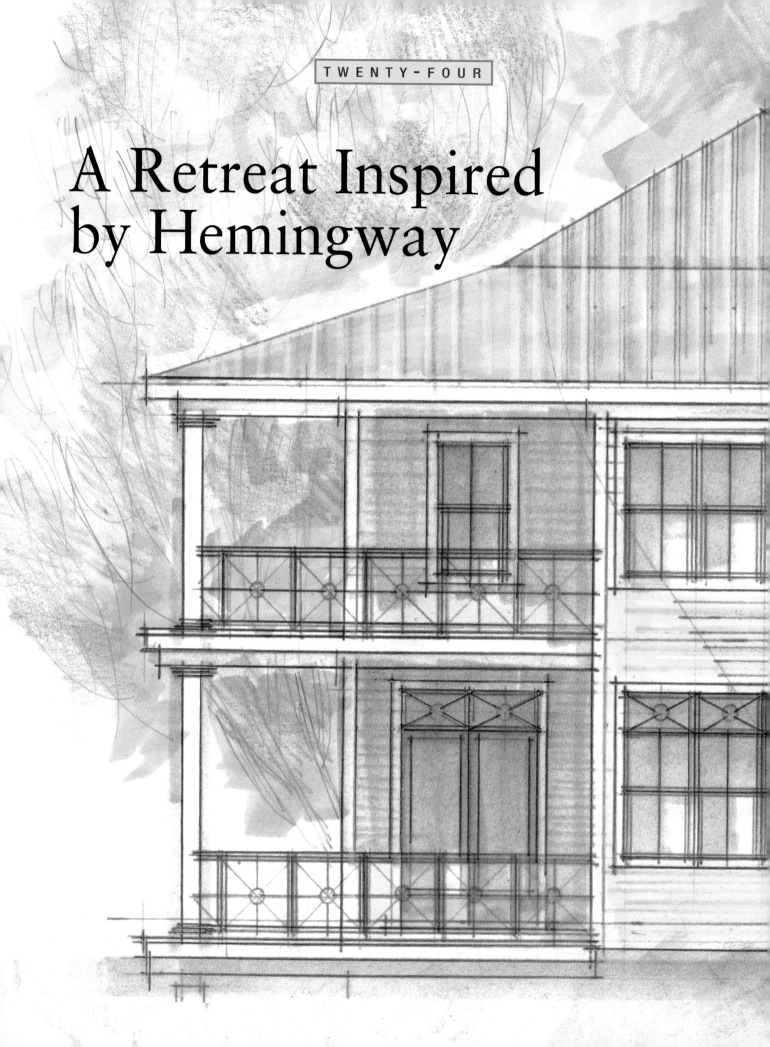

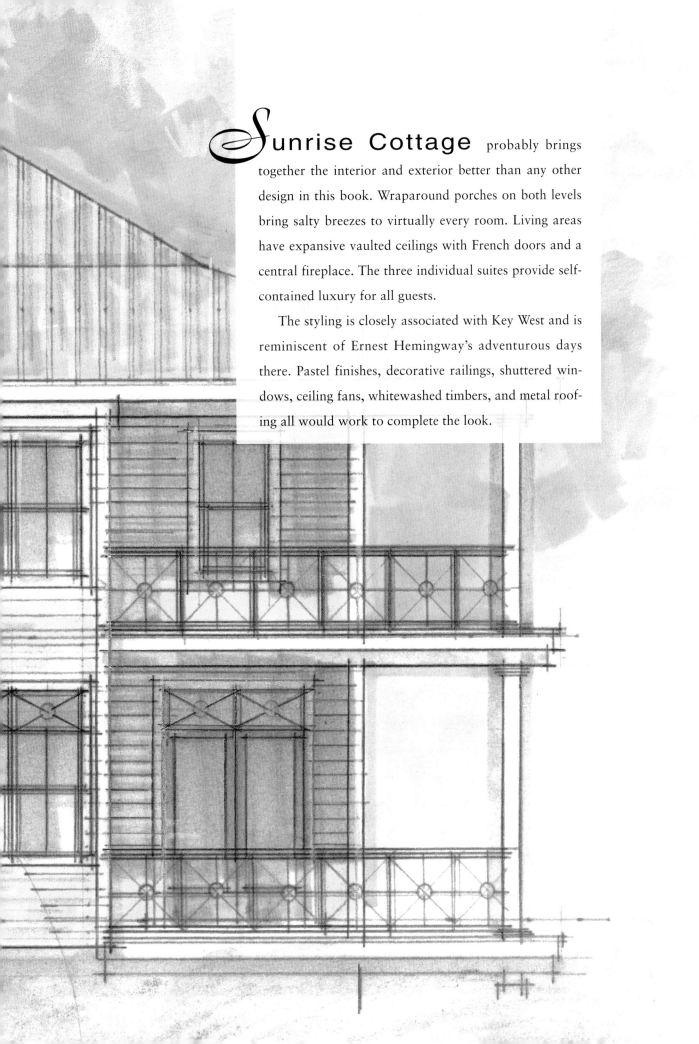

Sunrise Cottage

Sunrise Cottage probably brings together the interior and exterior better than any other design in this book. Wraparound porches on both levels bring salty breezes to virtually every room. Living areas have expansive vaulted ceilings with French doors and a central fireplace. The three individual suites provide self-contained luxury for all guests.

The styling is closely associated with Key West and is reminiscent of Ernest Hemingway's adventurous days there. Pastel finishes, decorative railings, shuttered windows, ceiling fans, whitewashed timbers, and metal roofing all would work to complete the look.

Building Style	Southern Coastal
Bedrooms	3
Bathrooms	3
First Floor Area	972 sq. ft.
Second Floor Area	555 sq. ft.
Total Floor Area	1,527 sq. ft.

Rear Elevation Features

- Covered rear entry
- Decorative entry door
- Fine column detailing

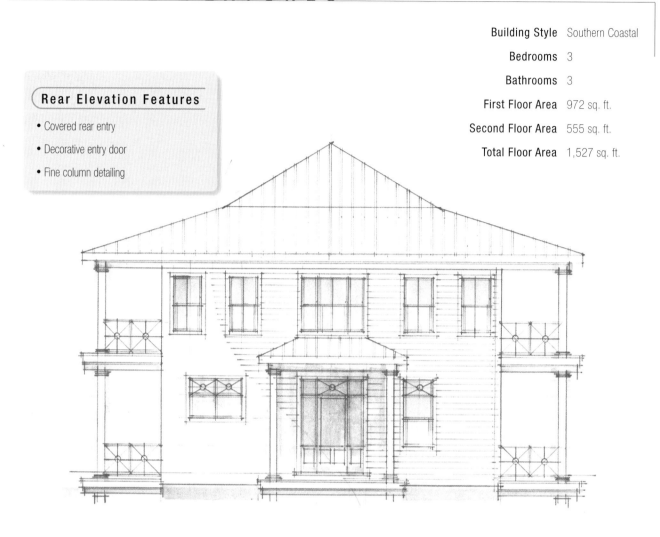

Visitors to the Keys

make evening pilgrimages to the beach for some of the most remarkable sunsets I have seen anywhere in the world. It must be the lavender, peach, lemon, pink, and blue of these scenes that inspire the architectural culture of the area.

Warmth and charm

are vividly associated with the Florida Keys. The open, breezy look of this wraparound balcony (left), similar to the one on Sunrise Cottage, is incredibly inviting. This style of building opens itself up to the beautiful views found in all directions.

Aged copper artifacts

and handiwork decorate a cottage with artful humor (above and left). Cottages are a fun place to experiment with a theme that may be dear to your heart. Some of my favorite collections have been twig art, hats, old photographs, antique skis, and snowshoes.

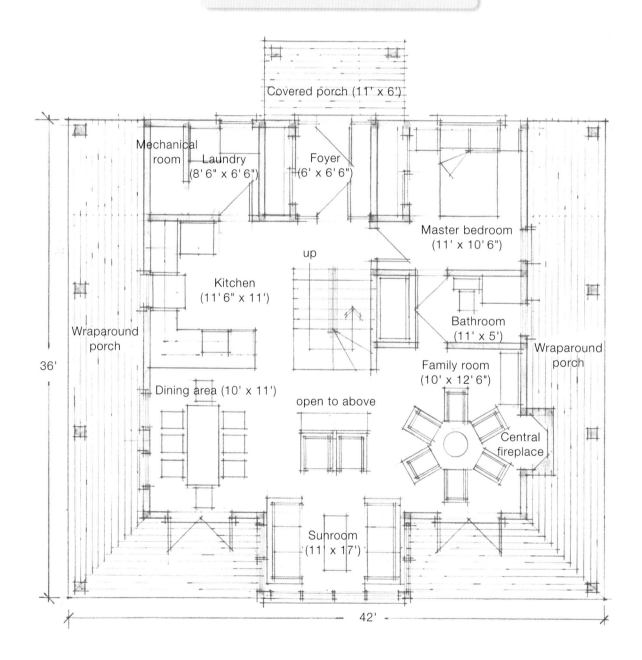

First Floor Features

- Covered rear foyer
- Full wraparound porch with walkouts from dining and living areas
- Sunroom
- Laundry/mechanical space
- Full master suite
- Central fireplace
- Vaulted ceiling over dining/living area

Covered porch (11' x 6')

Mechanical room

Laundry (8' 6" x 6' 6")

Foyer (6' x 6' 6")

Master bedroom (11' x 10' 6")

up

Kitchen (11' 6" x 11')

Bathroom (11' x 5')

Wraparound porch

Wraparound porch

Family room (10' x 12' 6")

Dining area (10' x 11')

open to above

Central fireplace

36'

Sunroom (11' x 17')

42'

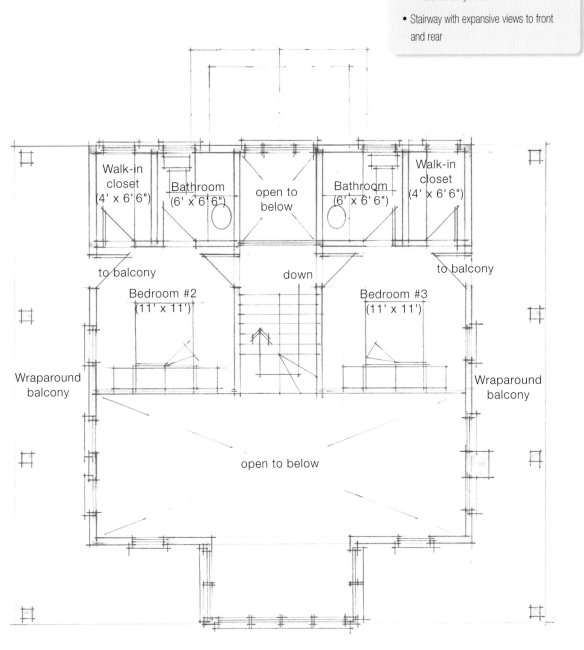

TWENTY-FIVE

A Welcoming Lighthouse

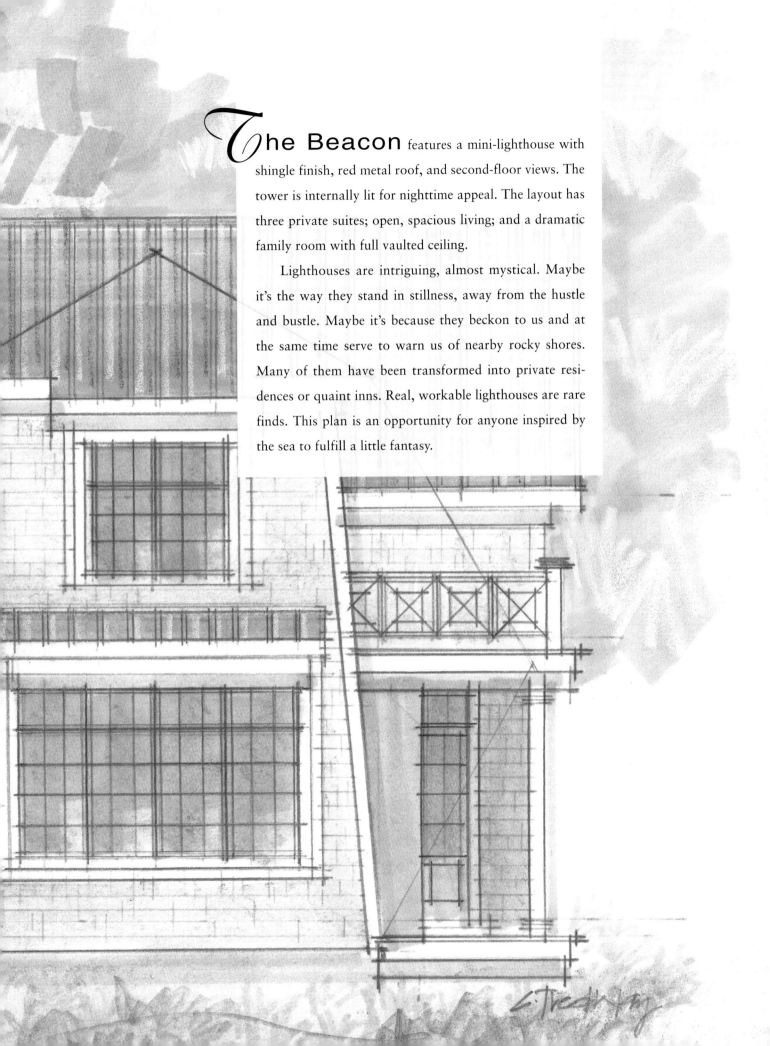

The Beacon features a mini-lighthouse with shingle finish, red metal roof, and second-floor views. The tower is internally lit for nighttime appeal. The layout has three private suites; open, spacious living; and a dramatic family room with full vaulted ceiling.

Lighthouses are intriguing, almost mystical. Maybe it's the way they stand in stillness, away from the hustle and bustle. Maybe it's because they beckon to us and at the same time serve to warn us of nearby rocky shores. Many of them have been transformed into private residences or quaint inns. Real, workable lighthouses are rare finds. This plan is an opportunity for anyone inspired by the sea to fulfill a little fantasy.

GENERAL FEATURES

Building Style	Specialty (Lighthouse)
Bedrooms	3
Bathrooms	1 full, 3 half
First Floor Area	968 sq. ft.
Second Floor Area	608 sq. ft.
Total Floor Area	1,576 sq. ft.

Front Elevation Features

- Lighthouse tower
- Walkout to second-level balcony
- Walkout from master suite
- Covered entry

Left Elevation Features

- Cheerful sunroom area
- Second-level windows in vaulted level above family room
- Generous windows in all bedrooms
- Decorative railings
- Expansive decks

Cupolas are defined

as light structures on a dome or roof, serving as a belfry, lantern, or belvedere. Over the centuries, they have served as:

- practical ventilation to barns, allowing hot air and fumes to escape
- towers on homes or light-houses whose lights call sailors in from the sea
- coverings for bells on churches or schoolhouses
- clock towers for city squares

- church tops rising skyward

Whatever its particular purpose, a cupola is a beacon. It tells us we are in a safe and familiar place. I think this is why we see them reincarnated once again on our recreational sites, in new uses with the same old message. Whether they function as a night-light or have a more symbolic function, as on the Beacon, they tell us we are home.

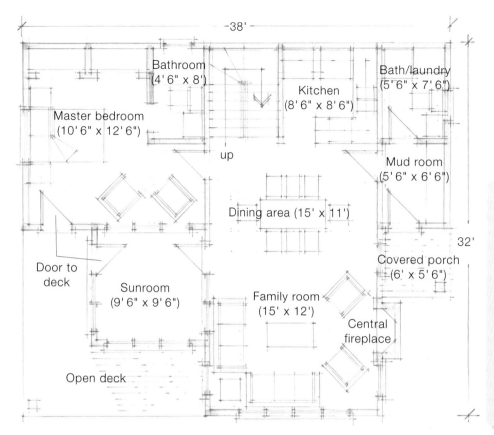

Bathroom
(4' 6" x 8')

Kitchen
(8' 6" x 8' 6")

Bath/laundry
(5' 6" x 7' 6")

Master bedroom
(10' 6" x 12' 6")

up

Mud room
(5' 6" x 6' 6")

Dining area (15' x 11')

Covered porch
(6' x 5' 6")

Door to
deck

Sunroom
(9' 6" x 9' 6")

Family room
(15' x 12')

Central
fireplace

Open deck

32'

-38'-

First Floor Features

- Open concept kitchen/dining area
- Master suite with private bath and walkout to deck
- Three-piece bathroom with laundry
- Mud room
- Family room with central fireplace and dramatic vaulted ceiling
- Sunroom with full glazing open to deck
- Covered entry

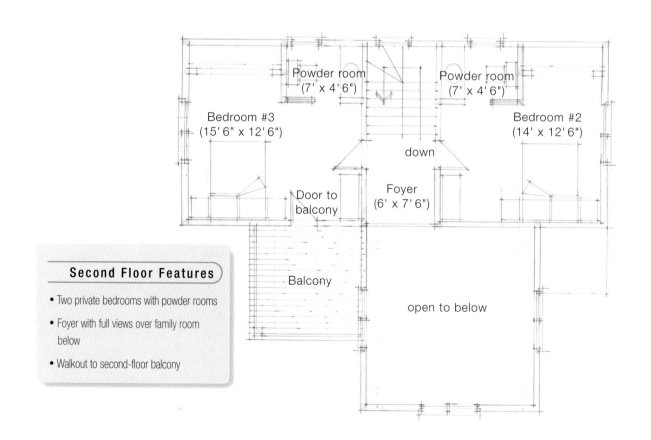

Powder room
(7' x 4' 6")

Powder room
(7' x 4' 6")

Bedroom #3
(15' 6" x 12' 6")

Bedroom #2
(14' x 12' 6")

down

Door to
balcony

Foyer
(6' x 7' 6")

Balcony

open to below

Second Floor Features

- Two private bedrooms with powder rooms
- Foyer with full views over family room below
- Walkout to second-floor balcony

The mechanical lifelines are crucial to the uninterrupted function of any cottage. Plumbing; electricity; heating/air conditioning; phone, data and satellite links; and even central vacuuming should all be considered in this "hidden" phase of construction. Although mechanical design is generally more simplified at a cottage than at a full-time home, one should allow for the added obstacles of remote access, environmental restrictions, and the probability of more frequent service interruptions.

▶ Plumbing

The plumbing system is the most delicate of all cottage services. Water can be drawn from natural sources, wells, and occasionally municipal services. The pressure from ruptured water systems can cause thousands of gallons of spillage in a short period of time, damaging both the structure and electrical servicing. Areas that experience winter freezing should take special care to empty all lines when the building is not in use. For added protection during cold weather I recommend heated water and sewage lines and duplicate lines in case of an unexpected blockage.

Conservation requirements are strict in most rural settings, and local authorities will determine the technical aspects of a private sewage system depending on its size, its occupancy capability, and local soil conditions. Modern technologies offer systems that reduce the size of a traditional septic bed.

▶ Electricity

When purchasing a cottage site, your first consideration should be the availability of electricity. Bringing high voltage lines to the site by pole, underground, or underwater can be expensive. A local certified electrician can assist you in determining the panel size and appropriate voltage for your service. Many cottages install backup generators for essential service in the event of extreme weather, falling trees, and power interruptions. Although high-tech generators are just around the corner, they are not yet common, and most cottages still rely on conventional wire services.

▶ Heating and Air Conditioning

Many cottages take a modest approach to heating and cooling, relying on natural ventilation, ceiling fans, and fireplaces to make modest climate adjustments. Full heating systems are essential to properties that are used year-round. Occasionally I have an industrious client who heats only with wood, but I caution against this approach as it requires steady maintenance and can put other services at risk.

Gas fireplaces are fairly new to the market as a viable heating source, but they are relatively inexpensive, can be set on a thermostat, and do not require a full system of ducting. As a moderate solution they are a great choice.

Full heating/air conditioning systems have similar requirements in a cottage and in a full-time residence. The furnace must be in a weather-secure location; this can be a challenge in cottages without basements. Ductwork and insulation should be installed during initial construction if you are considering a full system, as these types of renovations are usually not practical later.

Many areas require heat recovery ventilators in designs with vaulted ceilings. This system recirculates hot air during cold months and removes it during hot months.

▶ Phone, Data, and Satellite Links

When you are checking into the availability of electrical service, investigate the possibilities of phone service as well. Data and satellite links may seem to be extreme considerations for a recreational site, but advances in these technologies have made them common in even modest cottages. Kits can be installed by most electricians during the rough-in stage.

▶ Central Vacuuming

Central vacuuming is a bit of a luxury at a cottage, but it is inexpensive, easily concealed, and extremely helpful for cleanup after high-traffic weekends.

Glossary

Architrave. The milled trim around a door or window opening.

Bay Window. A projecting bay with straight sides and windows. Bays may be cantilevered or extended straight to the foundation level. Typically the space provides extra floor area or a window seat.

Bow Window. A curved bay window.

Bracket. A small projection that supports, or seems to support, a lintel or cornice.

Capital. A head, or top, of a column.

Cathedral Ceiling. A vaulted ceiling, as is common in churches.

Clapboards. Horizontal, overlapping boards covering the outside walls of a building. On older structures the overlap is 3 to 5 inches

Classical Architecture. Architecture used by the ancient Romans and Greeks, and subsequent styles based on it, such as Georgian, Federal, Greek Revival, Renaissance Revival, Italianate, and French Second Empire.

Clerestory Windows. Windows located high in a wall, such as immediately under the roof.

Column. A vertical pole or pillar supporting a roof or other structure.

Conduit. A pipe used to hold electrical cable in outdoor installation. Most local building codes demand that all outdoor cable be protected from weather by a conduit casing.

Corbel. Any projection from a masonry wall used for decorative effect and sometimes as a support.

Corner Boards. Narrow vertical boards that cover the corners of a wood frame house. The siding (usually shingles or clapboards) butts against the edges of the boards.

Cornice. The top portion of an entablature, usually molded and projecting from the wall. Any molded transition between a wall and a ceiling.

Course. A row of building material, such as brick, often positioned for decorative effect.

Cupola. A structure on a dome or roof, serving as a belfry, lantern, or ventilation source.

Curtain Wall. A light, non–load-bearing, weatherproof wall placed over the face of a building. Usually this is a metal grid that contains opaque panels. Curtain walls are an inexpensive way to hide a degenerated exterior wall.

Dado. The lower part of an internal wall; if the dado contains wooden panels, it is often referred to as the wainscot.

Dentil. One of the series of horizontal blocks resembling teeth found in the lower part of a cornice or used as interior molding.

Design Concept. An illustration graphically representing the characteristics of the building interior and exterior in a preliminary form.

Dormer. A structure projecting from a pitched roof and including a window or windows.

Eggshell. Having little or no gloss, producing a finish midway between semi-gloss and flat.

Elevation. A head-on drawing of the face of a building or part of a building, such as a wall. It does not attempt to show any perspective.

Enamel. Any paint or varnish drying to a very hard, smooth, usually glossy finish.

En suite. Type of bathroom that connects directly to a master bedroom.

Entablature. A horizontal member extending across the top of columns.

Fascia. A flat board nailed to the ends of the rafters at the eaves of a roof. The gutter system is often nailed to the fascia.

Flat. Without gloss or sheen.

Frieze. A decorative band, as along the underside of the soffit, forming a stringcourse on an outside wall.

Gable. The triangular area at the ends of a house between the eaves line and the roof peak.

Gambrel Roof. A roof having two pitches to provide more headroom beneath. Gambrel roofs have gable ends.

Half-bath. Any bathroom that does not have a tub or shower.

Hipped Roof. A roof with a pitch on all sides that does not contain any gable ends.

Jamb. The vertical sides of a door or window opening, typically made from stock nailed to the aperture studs.

Joist. A horizontal beam that supports a floor and/or ceiling. Joists can be made from a variety of products such as dimensional lumber, pre-engineered lumber, or steel.

Latex Paint. A paint with a latex binder that coalesces as water evaporates from the emulsion.

Leader. A vertical pipe used to conduct water from the roof gutter system to the ground. Sometimes known as a downspout.

Lintel. A horizontal beam (often stone, steel, or wood) placed over doors or windows. Lintels can be both structural and decorative.

Mansard Roof. A roof having two pitches to provide more headroom in the top floor of the house. Mansard roofs have no gables.

Masonry. Any solid material laid in small units, such as brick and stone.

Mass. The effect of a solid object seen from the outside. Mass has height, width, and depth.

Molding. A decorative band of material used in cornices and as trim around doors and windows. Outside a house, molding is likely to be made of wood or stone; inside it is usually plaster or wood.

Mullion. The vertical member between windows set close together.

Muntins. The horizontal and vertical strips of wood or metal that separate the panes of glass in a window.

O.C. On center. The distance between the center of two adjacent framing members.

Oil Paint. A paint in which a drying oil is the vehicle for the pigment.

Pane. The transparent panel made of glass or plastic that forms a window. Panes are held in place by sash frames and muntins.

Partition Wall. A wood-framed wall inside a house. It may be load-bearing or non–load-bearing.

Pediment. A low, triangular gable in classical architecture, created by the slopes of a roof over an entablature.

Perspective Drawing. A drawing of a building or its interior that conveys dimensional perspective.

Pilaster. A decorative flat or half-round column that appears to be partially embedded in a wall.

Pinned Connection. A slender rod driven through parts to keep them together. In cottage construction, the term most commonly refers to the connection of concrete to stone with an anchored rod.

Pitch. The angle of the slope of a roof. Pitch is typically identified by the distance traveled vertically for each 12 units traveled horizontally. For example, $^6/_{12}$ is a shallow slope, while $^{12}/_{12}$ is a much steeper slope.

Plan. A one-dimensional drawing representing a horizontal cross-section of a room or building, showing the positions of walls, doors, windows, stairs, etc.

Primer. A base coat applied to a surface to improve the adhesion of subsequent coats of paint or varnish.

Rafter. One of the sloping frame members that holds up a roof.

Riser. The vertical portion of a stair that holds up the tread.

Sash. The movable portion of a window, forming the outer frame around the glass pane or panes.

Semi-gloss. Having moderate luster. Also known as satin.

Shutters. Small wooden doors attached to the sides of windows, either inside or outside the cottage.

Siding. Narrow horizontal or vertical boards attached to the outside of a house to protect it against the weather. Siding can be wooden clapboard or shingles, or it can be made from materials such as vinyl, aluminum, fiberglass, or steel.

Sill. The lowest horizontal member in a window or door opening, constituting the bottom of its frame.

Skirting. The enclosure around the perimeter of an area that creates a visual or insulation barrier.

Sonotube. Trademark for a brand of cylindrical column formed of compressed paper. It is often filled with concrete on site to make support piers.

Space. The interior area of a structure. The outside of a cottage represents mass; the inside is space.

Stain. A solution of dye or a suspension of pigment applied to penetrate and color the wood surface without obscuring the grain.

Structural Wall. Any wall that supports part of the floor and roof load of a house. Structural walls either extend all the way to the ground or rest on beams supported by the foundation.

Stud. Any vertical framing member in a framed wall.

Surround. The molded trim around a door or window.

Topcoat. The final coat of paint applied to a surface. Also called finish coat.

Transom Window. A window directly above the horizontal crosspiece (transom) topping a door or window.

Tread. The horizontal members of a stair, supported by a riser.

Vapor Barrier. A material such as plastic, film, or foil applied to retard the transmission of moisture.

Waterproofing. A membrane or treatment applied to render a surface impervious to water.

Winder. A tapered stair tread. By using several winders in a stairway you can turn the stairway in another direction. If all of the treads are winders you have a spiral staircase.

Window. Panes of glass held in a sash, which slides or fits into a frame. The dividers between the panes are called muntins. If two side-by-side windows are separated by a wide vertical piece of wood, the divider is known as a mullion.

A Note about the Cottage Plans

The room dimensions and square footage indicated in the floor plans are approximate and for illustrative purposes only.

If you would like to order construction drawings for any of the cottages in this book, or if you would like more information about Catherine Tredway's firm Barn Owl Designs, visit their Web site at BarnOwlDesigns.com, or contact them directly at 1-888-BARNOWL.

Metric Conversion Chart		
When the measurement given is	To convert it to	Multiply it by
inches	centimeters	2.54
feet	meters	0.305
square feet	square meters	0.0929
miles	kilometers	1.6
pounds	kilograms	0.45
°F	°C	$°F - 32 \times {}^5/_9$

Index

Other Storey Titles You Will Enjoy

Small House Designs. This collection of award-winning designs for small houses is accompanied by expert commentary, specific technical data, and beautiful exterior photographs. 208 pages. Paperback. ISBN 0-88266-966-4.

New Compact House Designs. This book includes 27 award-winning designs for single-family homes of less than 1,250 square feet. Each design features a site drawing, floor plans, and elevation and section drawings. 192 pages. Paperback. ISBN 0-88266-666-5.

The Dock Manual, by Max Burns. This is the only book available devoted to planning, constructing, and maintaining residential docks on rivers, lakes, and oceans. 208 pages. Paperback. ISBN 1-58017-098-6.

Be Your Own House Contractor, by Carl Heldmann. The author tells you everything you need to know to manage any home construction project and save up to 25 percent or more on the total cost. Includes information on finding property, hiring good subcontractors, purchasing materials, and estimating costs. 160 pages. Paperback. ISBN 1-58017-374-8.

Rustic Retreats, by David and Jeanie Stiles. A complete guide to building sturdy, inexpensive, and beautiful backyard and woodland shelters. 160 pages. Paperback. ISBN 1-58017-035-8.

Garden Retreats, by David and Jeanie Stiles. Inspiring projects for outdoor living spaces, including a garden swing, rose arbor, gazebo, and potting shed. 160 pages. Paperback. ISBN 1-58017-149-4.

The Lawn & Garden Owner's Manual, by Lewis and Nancy Hill. The homeowner's ultimate landscape care and maintenance manual, this book allows you to rejuvenate neglected landscaping and keep your grounds beautiful and healthy throughout the year. 192 pages. Paperback. ISBN 1-58017-214-8.

Build a Classic Timber-Framed House, by Jack A. Sobon. Using actual plans, the author shows readers how to build a classic hall-and-parlor home. 208 pages. Paperback. ISBN 0-88266-841-2.

These books and other Storey books are available at your bookstore, farm store, garden center, or directly from Storey Books, Schoolhouse Road, Pownal, Vermont 05261, or by calling 800-441-5700. Or visit our Web site at www.storeybooks.com